MINIATURE
BOBBIN LACE

MINIATURE
BOBBIN LACE

ROZ SNOWDEN

GUILD OF MASTER CRAFTSMAN PUBLICATIONS LTD

First published 1998 by
Guild of Master Craftsman Publications Ltd,
166 High Street, Lewes,
East Sussex BN7 1XU

© Roz Snowden 1998

ISBN 1 86108 086 7

Photography by Zul Mukhida
Line drawings by John Yates

Frontispiece: Lacemaker's cottage
Designed by Ian Hunt Design
Typeface: Sabon
Origination by Master Image Ltd, Singapore
Printed and bound by Kyodo Printing (Singapore)
under the supervision of MRM Graphics, Winslow,
Buckinghamshire, UK

CONTENTS

ACKNOWLEDGEMENTS

My gratitude goes to all who have helped to make this book possible.

My thanks go to my husband Brian and sons Matthew, Daniel and Oliver, for their encouragement and help with the complexities of the computer.

Thanks also to Sheila Dobbie, for checking my spelling and grammar and for testing the patterns; to Liz Inman, Sarah Widdicombe, Bryony Benier and Andy Charman for their editorial help; to John Yates for producing the diagrams, and to Zul Mukhida for taking the photographs.

Many thanks to Pat Read and Sandi Wood, for their invaluable support.

Thanks to Harry Brackell for making the room boxes.

Finally, special thanks go to my students, who have worked the patterns and generously lent items for the photography: Christine Armstrong, Peggy Barnes, Rita Brackell, Carlyn Galvin, Ruth Gardner, Sylvia Gower, Sylvia Hobbs, Georgina Jackson, Carol Milner, Patricia Sumner, Sue Ticehurst, Jean Watson, Jane Webb, and Sue Wood.

INTRODUCTION

From an early age I have always made crafts, and over the years I became particularly intrigued by lacemaking. Seeing a class for bobbin lacemaking advertised in my local adult education centre, I enrolled and was quickly hooked. City and Guilds Creative Studies in Bobbin Lace quickly followed, and was successfully completed two years later. I was then introduced to the miniature world of dolls' houses, and so miniature lace was a natural progression. A few years later I started to teach bobbin lacemaking to a group of miniaturist friends, and this book is a result of those classes and much encouragement from my students, family and friends.

The book is aimed at all lacemakers, from the complete beginner to the more experienced, and includes a full range of projects in $\frac{1}{12}$th scale from simple, quick items that will take one or two evenings to complete, to miniature heirlooms which will keep you occupied for perhaps a month or two.

There are over 40 projects for you to try, all in $\frac{1}{12}$th scale. Each chapter is based on a different room in the dolls' house, and the patterns are not tied to any particular period in history. At the beginning of each chapter, a large photograph of the room shows all the projects *in situ*. Each project is shown with a pricking pattern, a diagram, and a photograph of the right side of the lace. (Lace is worked with the wrong side facing upwards.) The projects are graded for difficulty:

❀   Beginner's pattern

❀❀   Intermediate

❀❀❀   Experience needed

Torchon lace miniaturizes very well, so most of the designs are for this type of lace. Two designs in English Bedfordshire lace – for a lady's dress trimmings (see page 38) and a bell pull (see page 99) – are also included. Torchon lace is easy to make and understand. It is a geometric lace, easily plotted out on graph paper for designing. Bedfordshire lace is a more flowing lace characterized by 'plaits' and 'leaves', and the method for working these is explained in detail. Experienced lacemakers will notice that twists are missing from some of the techniques. This is simply because they are not needed at this small scale.

A list of lacemaking suppliers is provided at the back of the book.

I hope you will enjoy learning the techniques for producing successful miniature bobbin lace, and will spend many pleasurable hours making up a good selection of the projects for your own dolls' house.

CHAPTER ONE

MATERIALS
and EQUIPMENT

To start making lace you need the basic materials and equipment listed right, some of which are shown in Fig 1.1. Each item is fully described, and its uses explained, in the following pages. None of the equipment is expensive or difficult to handle, and everything is easily either made or acquired.

- Pillow
- Bobbins
- Pins
- Pricking card
- Pricker
- Thread
- Cover cloth
- Scissors
- Crochet hook

Fig 1.1 Some of the equipment you will need to make miniature bobbin lace.

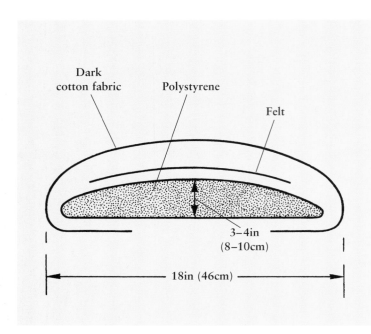

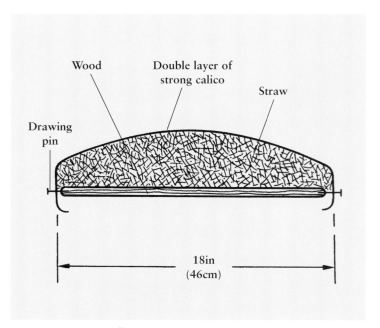

PILLOW

A pillow is the working surface for making bobbin lace. Pillows come in many shapes and sizes, but the following two pillows are adequate for working all the patterns in this book.

Until you know whether you enjoy lacemaking enough to invest in more permanent equipment, the easiest and cheapest way to make a pillow is from high-density polystyrene. This can be obtained from most builders' merchants and you will need a circular block approximately 18in (46cm) in diameter and 3–4in (8–10cm) deep. Shape the sides to a slight dome and place several layers of felt over the top to help protect the pillow. From plain, dark-coloured cotton fabric cut a circle approximately 24in (60cm) in diameter and hem around the edge. Leave a gap, and thread tape or elastic through the hem channel. Place the cover over the pillow, then pull up the tape underneath and secure (see Fig 1.2). Do not cut the tape:

Fig 1.2 A polystyrene pillow.

this will allow the cover to be removed for laundering.

A more traditional pillow can be made as follows. Cut a circle approximately 18in (46cm) in diameter from wood $^3/_8$in (1cm) thick. Cut two circles approximately 22in (56cm) in diameter from strong, closely woven calico. Place the fabric over the wood and attach the edge of the fabric around the side of the wood with drawing pins, leaving an opening. Roughly chop some straw (preferably oat straw, as it has softer stem joints, which is available from pet shops) and push it into the opening. Continue to pack in the straw, ramming it in to make the pillow as hard as possible. Try to achieve a firm, domed shape that will keep the pins firm and this will produce good quality lace (see Fig 1.3). Close the opening by pushing in more drawing pins around the edge of the calico, and cover the pillow with a gathered fabric cover as before.

Fig 1.3 A straw pillow.

BOBBINS

Bobbins are the tools with which you make the lace. Traditionally, they are made from either wood or bone, but now there are many bobbin makers able to supply good quality plastic bobbins for the beginner. There are many lovely bobbins available, but for miniature lace choose the finest and lightest.

Bobbins are approximately 4in (10cm) long, with a neck and head at one end and a spangle of beads at the other (see Fig 1.4). The thread is wound onto the neck and secured by a hitch in the thread over the head; when choosing bobbins, make sure the neck and head are really smooth as rough wood will catch on the thread. Bobbins are always wound in pairs and the number of pairs needed is given at the start of each pattern.

The spangle of glass beads on brass wire is there to achieve good tension through its weight on the thread, and to prevent the bobbins from twisting around while on the pillow, thereby twisting the thread.

Traditionally, a spangle had one large bead at the bottom, with three square-cut beads on either side (three round beads are perfectly acceptable). These are threaded onto brass wire (used because it does not rust) and onto the bobbin, with the ends hidden in the bottom bead (see Fig 1.5). Make the spangle small and neat.

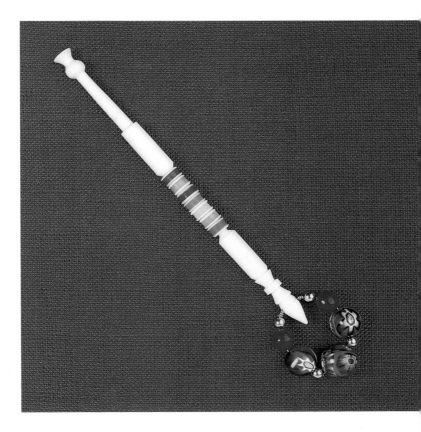

Fig 1.4 A bobbin, shown full-size.

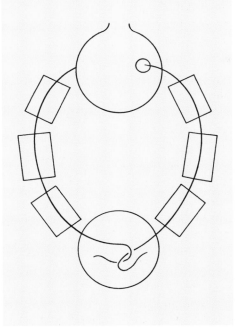

Fig 1.5 The anatomy of a spangle.

PINS

Use short, fine rustproof brass pins for lacemaking. Most of the patterns in this book use 30 x 0.55mm Newey pins, but for the really 'mini' laces, using 170/2 Egyptian gassed cotton thread, you will need to use extra-fine 17 x 0.45mm Duchesse pins, as the pinholes are really close together: using larger pins will not produce satisfactory lace. Both these pins are available from the suppliers listed on page 163.

Use a pincushion attached to the pillow by pins to keep your lacemaking pins readily available for use. Glass-headed pins are used for pinning cover cloths and securing bobbins (see page 8). Larger pins called dividers (hatpins are ideal) are used to keep the bobbins not in use to the sides of the pillow.

PRICKING CARD

Patterns in lacemaking are called prickings. Traditionally they were made from parchment and attached to the pillow by cloth tabs secured to both ends of the parchment. Nowadays, lacemakers use thin, brown glazed card available from lacemaking suppliers. As an inexpensive alternative, you could use the cardboard from a cereal box, covered with a matt-coloured, transparent adhesive film. This coloured film helps you to see the white threads and again is available from lacemaking suppliers.

Using a pricker (see below), the card is pricked with fine holes and then marked with a fine pen. As the pricking patterns in this book are so small, it is essential to use a really fine waterproof pen. For the coarser patterns, a 0.1 fine liner can be used; for the more intricate patterns, use a finer pen such as a

Rotring isograph 0.13 pen. These pens can be bought at good art or stationery shops.

An example of a simple pricking pattern is given on page 8.

PRICKER

A pricker is used to make the pricking. This is a small pin vice with a fine sewing needle inserted, leaving the pointed end protruding to a length of $\frac{5}{8}$in (15mm). A size 9 needle was used for all the prickings in this book. An easy way of making a basic pricker would be to insert a needle into a firm cork.

THREADS

The threads used for the patterns in this book are given at the start of each project. Traditionally, linen threads were used, but these are too coarse for miniature lace and cotton threads are used throughout. There are many threads available, and where possible I have given alternatives. For the simpler patterns, I have specified a suitable thread for beginners. For the more experienced lacemaker, substituting a finer thread will produce a more delicate effect.

The threads used to make up the projects in this book are:

- DMC Broder Machine 50
- Madeira Tanne 50 and 80
- Egyptian gassed cotton 120/2 and 170/2
- DMC Perle 12
- DMC Flower thread

Synthetic threads are not recommended because they are springy and the bobbins easily become unwound. Because of their high twist and polished surface, the threads do not bend sympathetically around the pins or give the soft hanging qualities desirable at this scale. They would also melt if ironed.

COVER CLOTH

A cover cloth is used while the work is in progress, to protect the pillow from the movement of the bobbins (see Fig 2.2 on page 8). Make up the cover from a square of dark-coloured cotton fabric which is slightly larger than the pillow. Hem it on three sides, and use the selvedged edge for the fourth side. Another cover cloth should be placed over the pillow when it is not in use, to protect the work from dirt and dust.

SCISSORS

You will need good quality, sharp embroidery scissors for cutting threads. You can also buy specialist lacemaking scissors which will help to prevent you from cutting into the lace when finishing off (see page 1).

CROCHET HOOK

A 0.4mm crochet hook is used to make 'sewings' when joining sections of lace together (see page 25).

ADDITIONAL EQUIPMENT

In addition to the basic materials and equipment described above, you may find the following items useful.

PIN LIFTER/PUSHER

This handy tool will help you to push in and pull out pins from the pillow without breaking your fingernails. It is readily available from lacemaking suppliers.

BOBBIN CASE

A bobbin case will keep your ready-wound pairs of bobbins tidy and untangled. The example shown in Fig 1.6 holds 24 pairs, but the design could be adapted to hold more or fewer pairs. When filled, the case can be rolled up and tied for security. Make each pocket approximately 3½ x 1½in (9 x 4cm) and the middle gap between the pockets approximately 2½in (6cm) wide.

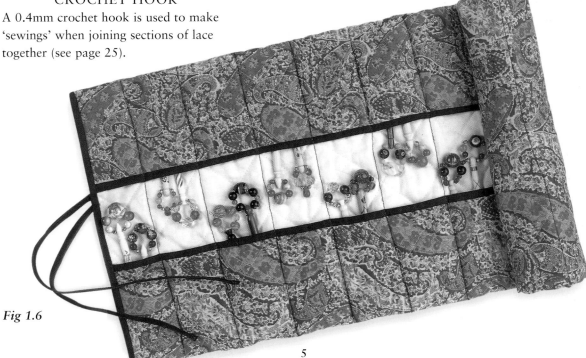

Fig 1.6

PILLOW BAG

A pillow bag is not a vital piece of equipment – a plastic carrier bag will do – but it is nice to have a purpose-made bag if you wish to travel with your equipment. Tailor the size of the bag to that of your pillow, allowing approximately 2in (5cm) extra all round. Join two pieces of fabric together with a zip or strip of Velcro on each side. Encase two strips of wood or thick card in fabric and gather the top edges of the bag onto these strips. Make shoulder straps or shorter straps for carrying (see Fig 1.7).

Another successful alternative would be to gather the bag onto ready-made handles, which can be purchased in needlework shops.

MAGNIFICATION AIDS

These are not strictly necessary, but because you will be working with small-scale patterns you may find them a great help. There are several different types available, including clip-on magnifiers that attach to spectacles and overhead magnifiers on a stand, which can be combined with a light and a small magnifier on a flexi-stem base that is pinned down onto the pillow. Choose whichever suits you best.

Fig 1.7 A pillow bag.

CHAPTER TWO

GETTING STARTED

This chapter explains how to prepare your pillow and bobbins to work your first pattern, and then how to work the two basic stitches of lacemaking so that you can work the beginner's braid.

PREPARATION

- Thread used: 8 pairs DMC Broder Machine 50
- If you have some experience in lacemaking, use Madeira Tanne 80

First, you need to make the pricking. Photocopy or trace Pattern 1 (Fig 2.1) from the book. Cut out this copy close to the pattern and then cut some pricking card slightly larger than this. Place the copy pattern on the card and pin both down onto a cork or polystyrene board with drawing pins at each corner. Do not use your pillow for pricking, as doing so will eventually destroy the surface. At each dot on the pattern, prick a hole with the pricker. Hold the pricker at 90° to obtain an accurate pricking. Push in approximately ³⁄₈in (1cm) of the needle – do *not* push the needle right in. A small ruler may help to keep your pricking line straight. It is essential that you try to be as accurate with your pricking as possible, because your finished work can only be as good as your pricking. Because the

pricking patterns are so small and the working lines so close to the pinholes, be very careful to prick only into the dots.

When you have finished pricking the holes, carefully remove the card and copy pattern from the board, leaving the drawing pins in place. Hold the card up to the light to check whether any holes have been missed. When you are satisfied with your pricking, remove the drawing pins and separate the card and copy pattern.

Using a fine liner pen, draw all the markings onto the pricking. If you do not wish to draw in the markings each time, instead of using the pricking method above you can place the copy pattern on the card and cover with transparent adhesive film. You will still need to prick each hole, but there will be no need to draw in the markings.

Place the pricking onto the pillow, in the middle and towards the top. The placement of the pricking on the pillow is important: too near the top, and you will find that you are stretching over the pillow to work; too near the bottom, and you will find the bobbins falling off the pillow. Pin the pricking to the pillow, pushing a brass pin right down at each corner. This pattern has two straight edges, so it is an 'insertion'. An 'edging' will have a straight edge and a patterned edge. Lace is always worked with the headside (patterned edge) on the left, and the footside (straight edge) on the right (see Fig 3.1 on page 17). Place the selvedge edge of the cover cloth over the bottom of the pricking and pin it down tightly at each end with glass-headed pins (see Fig 2.2).

You now need to wind the bobbins. Eight pairs are needed for working the first pattern. The first bobbin of the pair is wound from the reel of thread. Take the bobbin in your left hand and hold the end of the thread with your left thumb. Wind the thread over this end of thread onto the neck of the bobbin in a clockwise direction. For this pattern, wind approximately 48in (122cm) onto the bobbin (see Fig 2.3) and cut the thread. To secure the thread on the bobbin, you will need to make a double hitch onto the head of the bobbin. Still holding the bobbin in your left hand, wind the thread twice around your left thumb in a clockwise direction (see Fig 2.4). Place this thumb on the top of the head of the bobbin and slide the double loop onto the head (see Fig 2.5). This 'magical' double hitch (see Fig 2.6) secures the thread on the bobbin, but still allows it to be lengthened or

Fig 2.2 Lace pillow with work in progress.

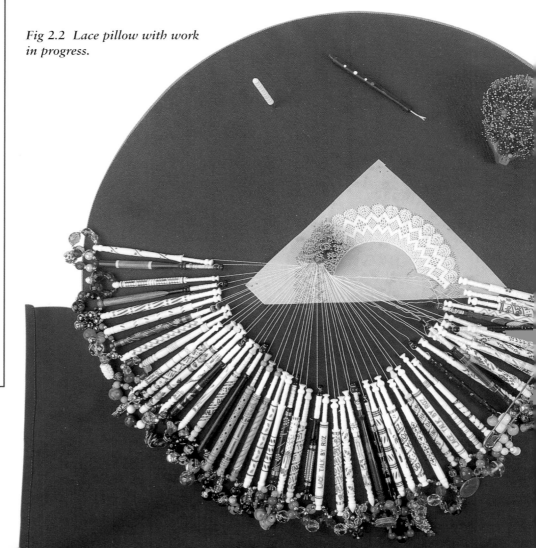

Fig 2.1 Pattern 1

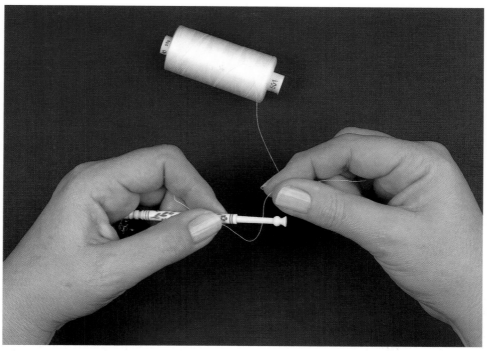

Fig 2.3 *Winding thread onto a bobbin.*

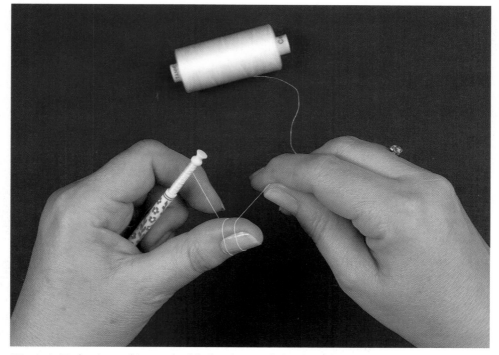

Fig 2.4 *To begin making a double hitch, wind the thread twice around your left thumb in a clockwise direction.*

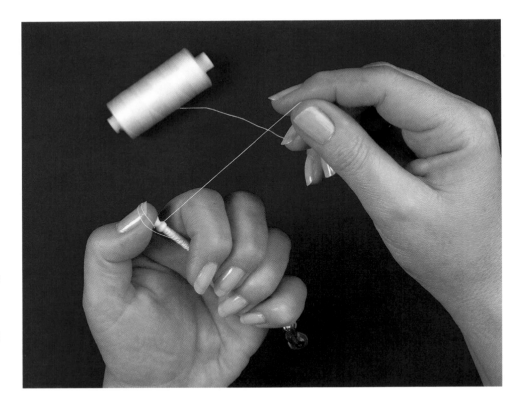

Fig 2.5 Making a double hitch: place your left thumb on the top of the bobbin and slide the double loop onto the head.

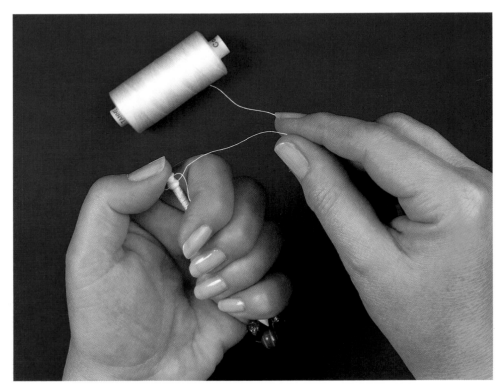

Fig 2.6 The double hitch secures the thread on the bobbin.

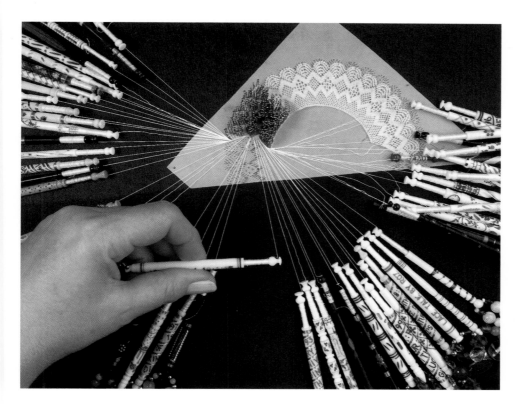

Fig 2.7 To lengthen the thread, hold the bobbin at 90° to the thread and twist the bobbin in a clockwise direction.

Fig 2.8 To shorten the thread, place a needle into the loop, pull out this loop, twist the bobbin in a anticlockwise direction and wind up the thread.

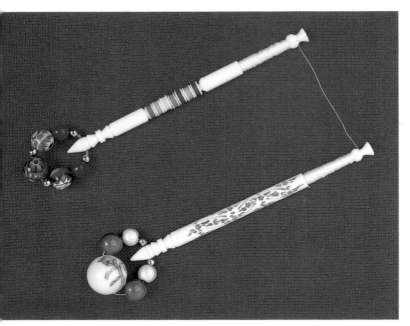

Fig 2.9 *A pair of bobbins wound with thread.*

Fig 2.10 *The correct sitting position.*

shortened if needed. To lengthen the thread, hold the bobbin at 90° to the thread and twist the bobbin in a clockwise direction to unwind to the required length (see Fig 2.7). To shorten the thread, place a needle into the loop (see Fig 2.8), pull out this loop and twist the bobbin in an anticlockwise direction to wind up to the required length.

Now wind the second bobbin. Take another bobbin in your left hand and hold the end of the thread with your left thumb. Wind back approximately 24in (60cm) of thread from the first bobbin and secure with a double hitch. Leave approximately 8in (20cm) of thread between the two bobbins (see Fig 2.9). Put this pair to one side and wind seven more pairs in the same way.

If you are using a pincushion, pin this to the top right of the pillow. Put a pin in each of the seven pinholes along the top of the pricking, sloping them back slightly to prevent the thread rising up the pins. Hang one pair of bobbins on each of these pins. These are called the passive pairs (warp threads) and they remain straight. Put a pin in the next hole on the left side, sloping it outwards slightly, and hang the remaining pair of bobbins on it. This is called the worker pair (weft thread) because it weaves in and out through the passive pairs, following the marked line.

Sit in a comfortable chair under good light. You may find it easier to sit at a table with your pillow at a slight angle (see Fig 2.10). Raise the back of the pillow with a book, or use a purpose-made bag approximately 8 x 5in (20 x 12.5cm), filled with polystyrene beads.

You are now ready to work your first pattern.

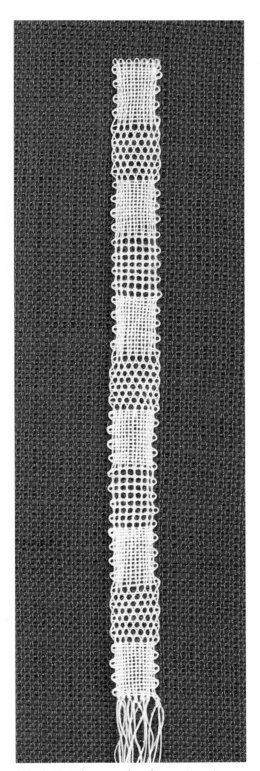

Fig 2.11 The completed practice piece.

BASIC STITCHES

The two basic stitches of lacemaking are cloth stitch and half stitch. The third stitch used in this braid is cloth stitch and twist, which is a combination of the other two. The terms you need to know are:

Cross Moving a left-hand bobbin over a right-hand bobbin.

Twist Moving a right-hand bobbin over a left-hand bobbin.

In the diagrams here, numbers refer to positions, not bobbins.

CLOTH STITCH (three movements) Start with the two pairs hanging on the left. Work one cloth stitch following Fig 2.12. Note that you will be working with only two pairs (four threads) at a time. Push the left pair away to the left and bring down the next pair from the right. Work another cloth stitch. Repeat

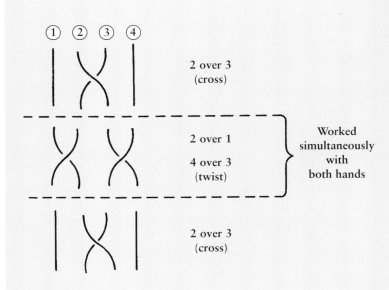

Fig 2.12 Cloth stitch.

13

this across all the passive pairs. Twist the worker pair on the right, right over left – this is shown on the diagrams as a short dash across the thread line. Put a pin in the next hole down on the right, under the worker pair. This is called 'pinning-up' (see Fig 2.13) and is expressed in the project instructions as 'pin up at X' or 'put up pin X'. Tension all the threads by gently stroking the bobbins; better lace will be produced if you can maintain good tension.

The worker pair now returns to the other side in exactly the same way as before: you do not have to reverse the stitch because you are working in the opposite direction. Twist the worker pair (pair on left) right over left, and pin under the worker pair into the next pinhole down on the left.

Continue working cloth stitch, practising the rhythm of the stitch, until you are more confident with working it. Remember to twist the worker pair every time a pin is put in. Try to watch the work in progress rather than the

bobbins. This way, you are more likely to catch any mistakes before you go too far. As you work, give yourself plenty of space and push the bobbins not being worked to either side.

Now change to the next stitch.

HALF STITCH (two movements)
Starting on the left as before, work one half stitch following Fig 2.14. Push the left pair away to the left and bring down the next pair from the right. Work another half stitch. Repeat this across all the passive pairs. You will see from working this that there is only one worker thread, whereas in cloth stitch there are two. When you have worked through all the passives, pin up under the worker pair on the right.

Continue working half stitch, tensioning the work each time you pin up. Try not to leave your work halfway across a row: when you are learning, it is easy to get lost. If you do, undo the last row back to the pin and start again, making sure that the passive pairs are still twisted right over left.

As this is a practice piece, you may now choose which stitches to work. I worked another block of cloth stitch, and then changed to cloth stitch and twist.

CLOTH STITCH AND TWIST
(DOUBLE STITCH)
(four movements)
Start on the left and work one cloth stitch and twist following Fig 2.15. Push the left pair away to the left and bring down the next pair from the right. Work another cloth stitch and twist. Repeat across all the passive pairs. Pin up on the right under the worker pair. Continue practising this stitch, remembering that it is not reversed as it works to and fro.

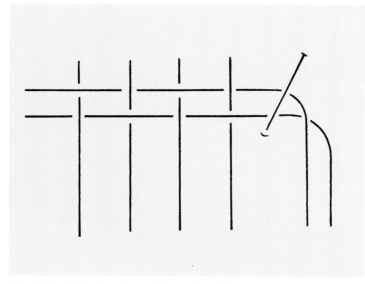

Fig 2.13 Twisting the worker pair and pinning up.

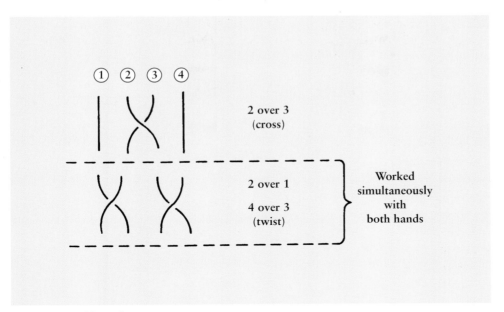

Fig 2.14 Half stitch.

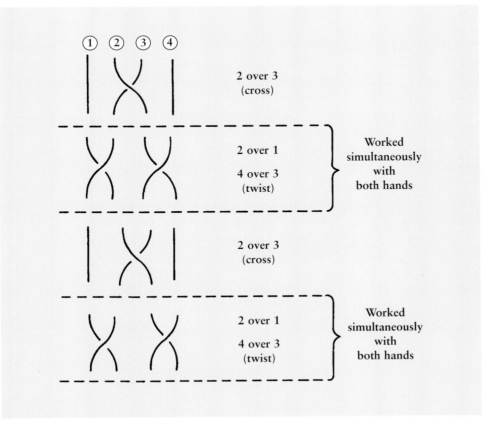

Fig 2.15 Cloth stitch and twist.

– TIP –

It is not necessary to keep all the pins in as you work down, but leave at least a 2in (5cm) depth of pins above the work. Remember that edge pins should be sloped outwards and the middle pins backwards, to help prevent the lace rising off the pillow.

SECURING WORK IN PROGRESS

If you want to travel with your pillow while work is in progress, the cover cloth can be used to 'put the pillow to bed'. Stretch some ³⁄₄in- (2cm-) wide elastic over the bobbins, and pin down between them using glass-headed pins. Push the pins flush into the pillow, taking care not to put them through the pricking card. (Anchoring the bobbins is important to avoid tangled threads – another method of securing them is to use knitting stitch-holders instead of elastic – see page 1.) Fold the bottom edge of the cover cloth upwards to cover the bobbins and lace, and pin it down.

FINISHING

At the end, tie off each pair individually with three knots (see Fig 2.16) and cut the threads to approximately 2in (5cm). Leave the lace to settle for 24 hours on the pillow (this is particularly important with the really 'mini' laces), then carefully take out the pins. Cut the ends of the threads short, trying not to cut into the knots. Lightly dab the cut ends with PVA glue or Fraycheck, and fold them back to the wrong side of the lace (the side facing you while the lace was on the pillow). Using glue is frowned upon in the 'big lace' world, but I think it is acceptable in the 'mini' world. Note that all the photographs of finished lace are shown with the right side uppermost.

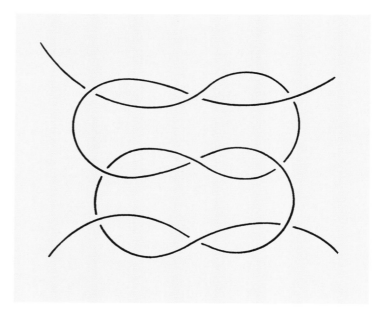

If you are mounting this practice piece onto fabric (see page 162), use the thread chosen for making the lace in your sewing needle. Although a practice piece, this beginner's braid can still be put to good use. I have decorated a little hat (see Fig 4.1 on page 31), and used it as an insertion in a petticoat or apron (see Fig 8.1 on page 104). Do not be discouraged if you feel that your first attempt is disappointing, but put it to good use somewhere in your dolls' house.

Now that you have finished your first piece of lace and gained some confidence, you can progress to working other patterns in the book. I suggest that you work the first pattern in each chapter, before progressing to the more complex designs.

Fig 2.16 Tying off pairs: knot three times.

CHAPTER THREE

STITCHES
and TECHNIQUES

This chapter explains how to work the stitches used in the beginner's patterns in this book, all of which incorporate cloth stitch, half stitch, and cloth stitch and twist. It also explains the basic techniques you will need to help you complete the patterns. Fig 3.1 illustrates some of the lacemaking terms, stitches and techniques used in this book. Additional stitches and techniques used for some of the more complex projects are described and illustrated in Chapter 10.

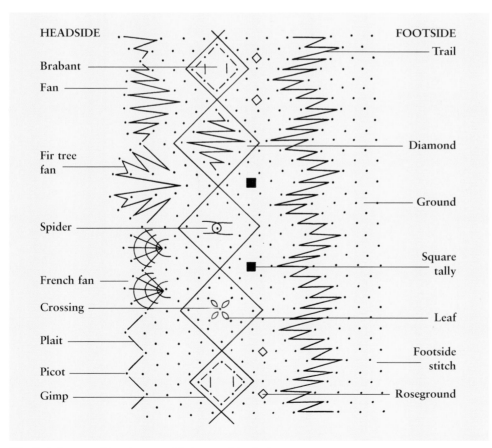

Fig 3.1 Lacemaking terms, stitches and techniques.

LACEMAKING TERMS

There are two different types of bobbin lace:

Continuous (Straight) Lace where the ground and motifs are all made at the same time. All the patterns in the book are for this type of lace.

Non-continuous Lace where the motifs are made separately and then joined together.

Lace is always worked with the headside (patterned edge) on the left, and the footside (straight edge) on the right.

While working on the pillow, the wrong side of the lace is uppermost. Note that the photographs of finished pieces of work in this book show the right side of the lace uppermost. Also, many of the pieces are shown prior to being finished off and still have passive pairs of threads hanging down.

STITCHES

TORCHON GROUND (Fig 3.2)

This ground stitch is worked in diagonal rows, with pairs coming to each pinhole at an angle of 45°. Each pinhole is worked with two pairs. Work the stitch as follows:

Half stitch, pin, half stitch.

TORCHON FOOTSIDE (Fig 3.3)

Work up to the last two pairs at the edge. The worker pair must now have a twist on it. Work a cloth stitch and twist out through the two edge pairs and put up a pin to the left of the last two pairs worked (this is called pinning up under two). Cover the pin with a cloth stitch

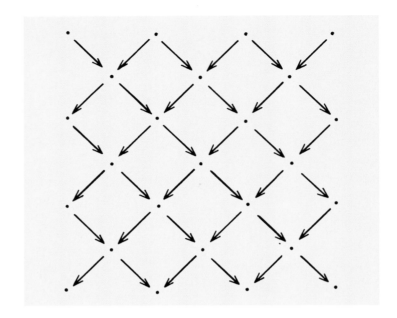

and twist. Work back with the left pair from the pin as the new workers. Working this stitch gives a firm, straight edge to the lace. If needed, this edge can be attached to the fabric (see page 162).

Fig 3.2 Torchon ground.

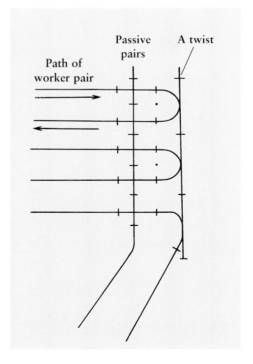

Fig 3.3 Torchon footside.

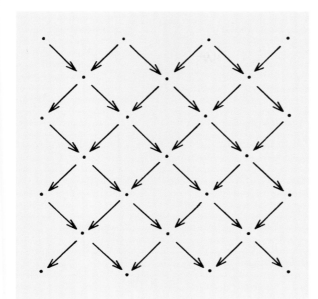

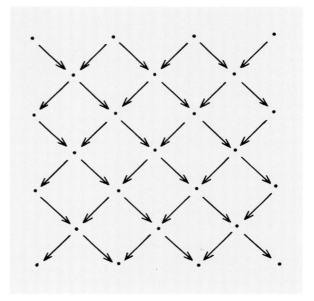

DOUBLE STITCH GROUND
(Fig 3.4)

This ground stitch is worked in diagonal rows with pairs coming to each pinhole at an angle of 45°. Each pinhole is worked with two pairs. Work the stitch as follows:

Cloth stitch and twist, pin, cloth stitch and twist.

PINHOLE GROUND (Fig 3.5)

This ground stitch is worked in diagonal rows with pairs coming to each pinhole at an angle of 45°. Each pinhole is worked with two pairs. Work the stitch as follows:

Half stitch, pin, half stitch and twist.

CLOTH OR HALF STITCH
DIAMOND (Figs 3.6 and 3.7)

Starting at pin **1**, take two pairs into the pin from the ground as indicated in Fig 3.6. Take one pair from the ground into the diamond at pinholes **2** to **7** and leave one pair out (to be taken back into

the ground) at pinholes **6** to **12**. Note that at pinholes **6** and **7** a pair is taken in and then left out immediately. Always start to work the diamond in the same direction: it does not matter which direction, but be consistent on each piece of lace. You must always end at the

Fig 3.4 ABOVE LEFT
Double stitch ground.

Fig 3.5 ABOVE RIGHT
Pinhole ground.

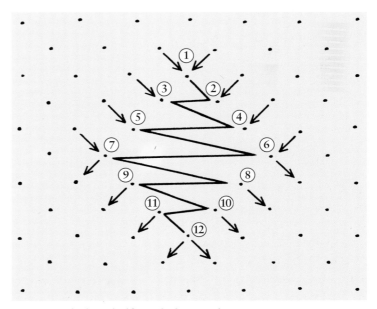

Fig 3.6 Cloth or half stitch diamond.

Fig 3.7 Cloth or half stitch diamond as shown on the pricking.

bottom pin with two pairs; if not, you will know that you have forgotten to take in or leave out a pair somewhere.

All cloth or half stitch shapes are worked on the same principle.

CLOTH OR HALF STITCH FAN
(Figs 3.8 and 3.9)

Take one pair from the ground into the fan at pinholes **2** to **5** and leave one pair out (to be taken back into the ground) at pinholes **5** to **8**. Note that at pinhole **5** a pair is taken in and then left out immediately. Try to achieve nicely curved passives with no large loops on the outside edge. When working the fan in half stitch, work the outside edge pair in cloth stitch and twist to give the edge some strength – half stitch is a flimsy, open stitch which is not particularly firm at the edges.

Fig 3.8 Cloth or half stitch fan.

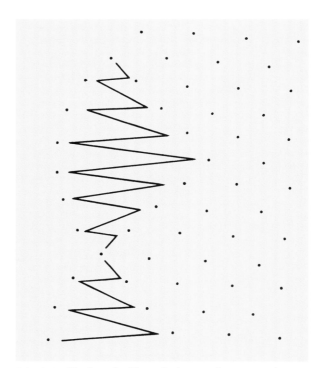

Fig 3.9 Cloth or half stitch fan as shown on the pricking.

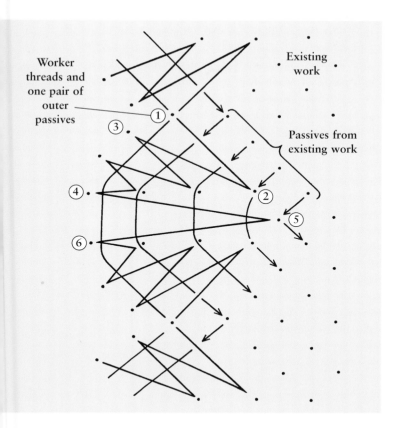

Worker threads and one pair of outer passives

Existing work

Passives from existing work

Fig 3.10 Fir tree fan.

FIR TREE FAN (Figs 3.10 and 3.11)
This fan may vary in size but six pairs are used in this example: two pairs on pin **1** (workers and outer passives) and four pairs coming in from existing work.

Take the workers to the right through four pairs in cloth stitch and twist and put up pin **2**. Return to the left through four pairs in cloth stitch and twist and put up pin **3**. Continue working through one pair less on each of the next two rows until pin **4** is put up. Work to the right through five pairs in cloth stitch and twist and put up pin **5**, then work back to the left through five pairs to pin **6**.

The second half of the fan is a mirror image of the first. When working the second half of the fan, tension the passive pairs carefully so that they curve

around to 'mirror' the first half of the fan. Each time an outside pin is put up, hold the worker pair in your left hand and pull the passives around to the right with the other hand.

FRENCH FAN (Figs 3.12 and 3.13)
This example of a French fan has three passive pairs. Other fans may have more, but the principle of working is the same.

1 Work the worker pair hanging left from pin **1** to the right in cloth stitch and twist through two pairs. Work the next pair in cloth stitch and put up pin **2** (the pivot pin).

2 Work to the left through one pair in cloth stitch, twist the workers and work to the left through two pairs in cloth stitch and twist. Put up pin **3**.

Fig 3.11 Fir tree fan as shown on the pricking.

3 Work to the right through two pairs in cloth stitch and twist, and one pair in cloth stitch.

4 Take the workers in your right hand and take them around the pivot pin **2** in a clockwise direction.

5 Work back to the left through one pair in cloth stitch, twist the workers and work to the left through two pairs in cloth stitch and twist. Put up pin **4**.

6 Continue in this way until pin **5** is put up. Do not cover the pin.

7 Continue with the ground stitches. Once pin **6** is put up, remove the pivot pin **2** and tension the fan by gently pulling the worker pair at pin **5** and the left pair at pin **6**. This will flatten the loops at the base of the fan.

SPIDER (Figs 3.14 and 3.15)
This example is a simple spider with two legs from left and right. Other spiders may have more legs, but the principle is the same.

The spider is worked with the four pairs coming from pins **1**, **2**, **3** and **4**. Twist all

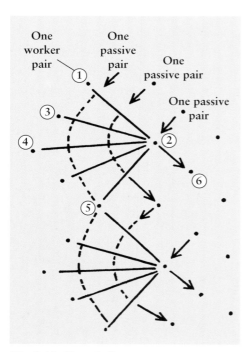

Fig 3.12 French fan.

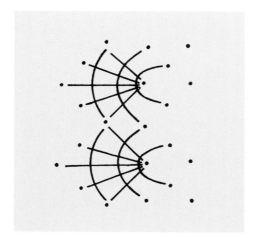

Fig 3.13 French fan as shown on the pricking.

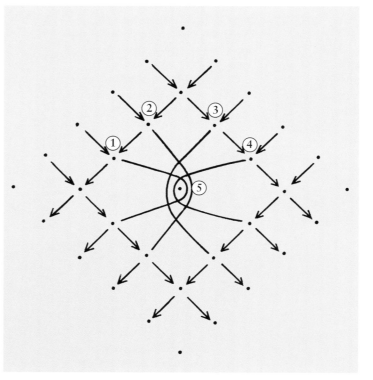

Fig 3.14 Spider.

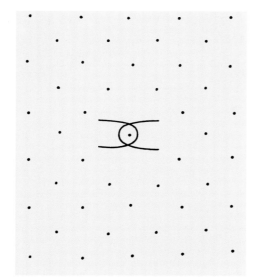

Fig 3.15 Spider as shown on the pricking.

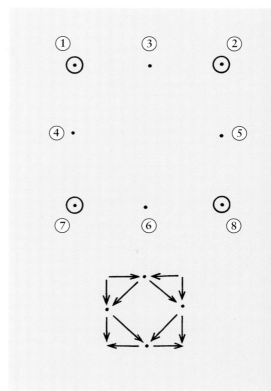

Fig 3.16 Roseground 1.

pairs three times. Work the pair at **2** through two pairs to the right in cloth stitch. Work the pair at **1** through two pairs to the right in cloth stitch. Note that the two pairs from pins **1** and **2** have worked through the two pairs from pins **3** and **4**. Put up pin **5** between the two centre pairs. Work the two left pairs through the two right pairs in cloth stitch as before. Twist each pair three times.

Try to keep the tension even throughout – the body of the spider should be flat.

ROSEGROUND 1
(Figs 3.16 and 3.17)

Work this stitch in number order (four pairs used):

Numbers **1** and **2** – cloth stitch and twist. *No pin.*
Pinholes **3**, **4**, **5** and **6** – half stitch, pin, half stitch.
Numbers **7** and **8** – cloth stitch and twist. *No pin.*

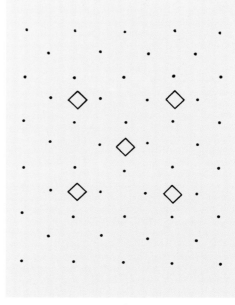

Fig 3.17 Roseground 1 as shown on the pricking.

Techniques

HANGING PAIRS SIDE-BY-SIDE
(Fig 3.18)

Hang two or more pairs on a pin in pairs.

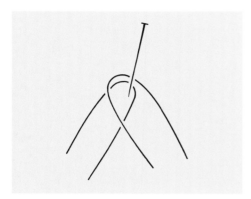

Fig 3.18 Hanging pairs side-by-side.

HANGING PAIRS OPEN (Fig 3.19)

Hang two or more pairs on a pin, one inside the other.

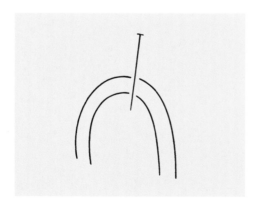

Fig 3.19 Hanging pairs open.

SUPPORT PINS

These pins are put into the pillow above the work to hold pairs of bobbins that are waiting to be brought into the work. Once the work is established, these pins are removed and the loops of thread are pulled down.

COVERING A PIN

When two pairs are worked together and a pin is put between them, this pin is usually covered by working together the same two pairs, in the same stitch as was used before the pin.

THROWING BACK PAIRS

When pairs are not needed in the work, lay them back to the top, over the work, to be cut off later. Never throw back two threads side by side, but stagger them. A knot must *never* be worked into the lace: if a knot appears, it *must* be thrown back. Lay the thread back and around a temporary pin above the work. Bring the thread back down into position in the work and continue working. When the lace is off the pillow, cut this loop close to the work.

BROKEN THREADS

When a thread breaks, it need not be a disaster. Use a weaver's knot to join the threads together – many lacemakers call this the 'magic knot' (see Fig 3.20). Make a slip knot (the knot used at the beginning of knitting) with the bobbin

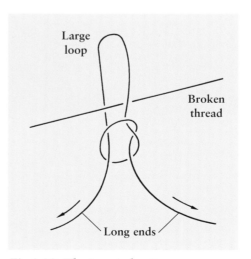

Fig 3.20 The 'magic knot'.

thread. Put the broken thread through this loop. Now slowly pull the two ends of the bobbin thread apart until the knot clicks onto the broken thread. You may need a friend to help you at this stage by holding the broken thread down onto the pillow while you click the loop onto the thread. If it does not click the first time, try again. The thread is now secure. Cut the ends short, and continue with the work. Throw the knotted thread back at a convenient place, by laying the thread around a temporary pin above the work. Bring the thread back down into the work and continue.

ADDING IN PAIRS

Put in a temporary support pin above the work. Put the new pair around this pin and hang the bobbins down into the work where it is needed. After a few stitches have been worked, remove the temporary support pin and pull the loop of thread down to the work.

SEWINGS

Sewings are made to join two sections of lace together. Push down flush to the pillow any pins that may be in the way. Lengthen the threads on the bobbins and start at the footside edge. Remove the pin and insert the crochet hook down into the loop made by the pin. Take the pair of bobbins that need to be sewn in, and pull through one of the threads to form a loop. Pass the other bobbin of the pair through this loop. Replace the pin and pull the pair tight up to the pin. Tie three knots close up to the pin with this pair (see Fig 2.16, page 16). If you are completing a square or circle, repeat this across the lace. Cut the threads long, and when the lace is off the pillow, cut them close to the work.

TRAIL (Figs 3.21 and 3.22)

A trail is a ribbon or 'path' of either cloth stitch or half stitch.

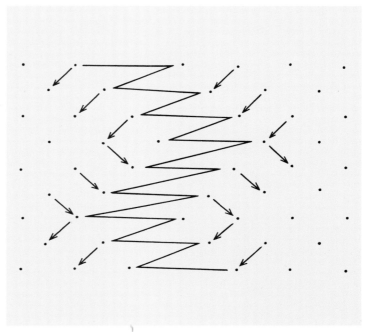

Fig 3.21 A trail.

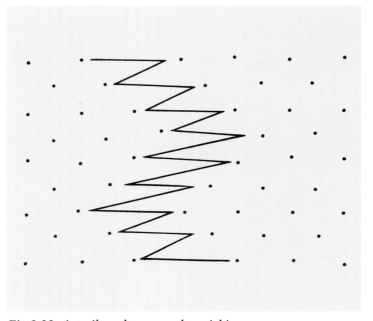

Fig 3.22 A trail as shown on the pricking.

GIMPS (see Figs 3.23 and 3.24)
These are thicker threads that surround
and outline parts of the pattern. Make
two twists on the pair before and after
the gimp thread has passed through.
Work gimp as follows:

Gimp going left to right – under first
thread, over second thread.
Gimp going right to left – over first
thread, under second thread.

*Fig 3.24 Gimp
threads as shown
on the pricking.*

Fig 3.23 Gimp threads.

FURTHER STITCHES AND TECHNIQUES

Additional stitches and techniques are
used for some of the more complex
designs in the book, and these are
explained in Chapter 10.

TOP LACEMAKING TIPS

1 Handle the threads as little as
possible, to keep them clean.

2 Work the ground in diagonal rows
from top to bottom. *Never work 'uphill'.*
When starting a pattern on a straight
line, build up the ground to the diagonal
line.

3 If the piece of lace is to be joined into a circle or square, start on a diagonal line at a point where the join will be least obvious, such as at the side of cloth shapes or fans, or alongside gimps.

4 Do not forget to remove support pins and pull down the looped thread.

5 Watch the work, not the bobbins. Mistakes can then be rectified as they happen.

6 To help yourself understand a new technique, practise with a thick thread and large pins.

7 To prevent the crochet hook rolling off the pillow, tuck the end under the edge of the cover cloth, to one side of the pillow.

8 When working large projects where the bobbins may run out of thread, wind them with different lengths so that they do not all run out at once.

9 After a new thread spool has been opened, tuck the label inside for future reference.

10 Always keep your samples and make notes, so that any mistakes can be avoided in the future.

11 Calculating how much thread to wind on a bobbin for a particular pattern is very difficult. Because many of my patterns use the same thread, I wind the bobbins full, singly, then knot them together in pairs and wind the knot back onto one of the bobbins. This knot is easily removed when it appears near the work (see page 24). If you are winding bobbins for one pattern only, roughly four times the length of the finished lace will be needed on each bobbin, although this will vary according to the stitches

being worked. Remember that the worker pairs in trails and fans will require more thread.

12 To calculate how much straight lace is needed to fit around a square or circle, draw out the finished article and measure around the outside edge. Add a little more to allow for stretch in the fabric (see Fig 3.25).

13 If a worker bobbin is running out of thread, it must first be changed with a passive pair, before it is refilled with thread. The easiest and less conspicuous way of doing this is to twist the empty bobbin with a passive bobbin as the workers pass around a pin (the worker thread now becomes a passive thread). With care, this will not show in the work. Work a few rows with the new worker bobbin. Rewind the empty bobbin, knot it to the old thread, and throw back the knot around a pin above the work (see page 24).

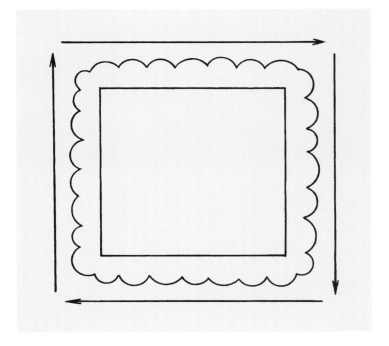

Fig 3.25 To calculate the length of straight lace required to fit around a square (or circle), measure all around the outside edge.

The
PROJECTS

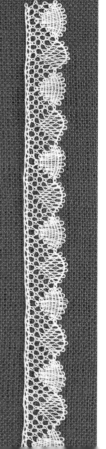

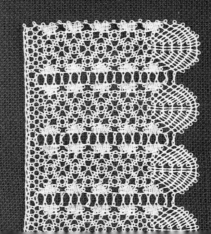

Fig 4.1

Hat WITH
FIR TREE FLOWER

FINISHED SIZE ¹³⁄₁₆in (2cm) diameter

I have used this edging to make a small flower to decorate a hat. It could also decorate a dress or perhaps a special birthday present parcel. Used as a straight edging, it would look pretty on a dress.

MATERIALS

9 pairs DMC Broder Machine 50

ALTERNATIVE THREAD
Madeira Tanne 50

STITCHES USED

Torchon ground	see page 18
Torchon footside	see page 18
Fir tree fan	see page 21

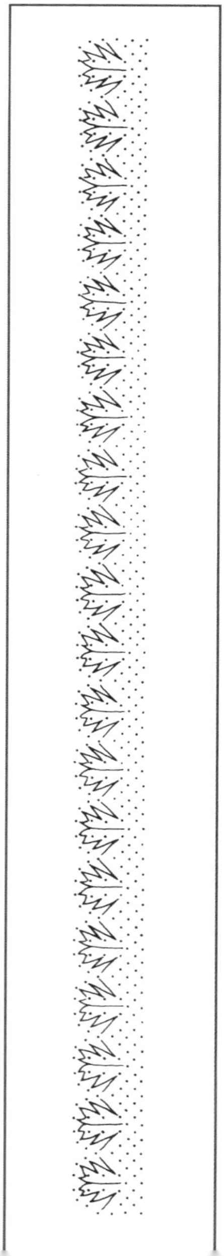

Fig 4.2

METHOD

1 Hang two pairs open on pins **1**, **2**, **3** and **4**. Twist each pair once. Cover pins **1** and **4** with cloth stitch and twist, and cover pins **2** and **3** with half stitch.

2 Hang one pair on a support pin above the work and bring down as shown in Fig 4.4.

3 Work a Torchon ground stitch at pin **5** with pairs from pins **2** and **3**.

4 With the left pair at pin **4**, work through the pair on a support pin in cloth stitch and twist.

5 With this pair and the right pair from pin **3**, work a Torchon ground stitch at pin **6**.

6 Work the right pair from pin **6** through two pairs to the right in cloth stitch and twist and pin up at **7** under two pairs (to the left of the last two pairs worked) (footside edge). Cover the pin with cloth stitch and twist. *Remove the support pin and pull down the spare thread.*

7 Following Fig 4.4, work Torchon ground stitches at pins **8** and **9**, and a footside edge stitch at pin **10**.

8 The right pair hanging from pin **1** is the worker pair for the fir tree fan, which is worked now.

9 When the fan is complete and you have put up pin **11** under the worker pair, leave the pin uncovered.

10 *Work Torchon ground stitches at pins **12** to **15**, and footside edge stitch at pin **16**. Repeat this sequence of stitches

Fig 4.3 LEFT *Pattern 2*

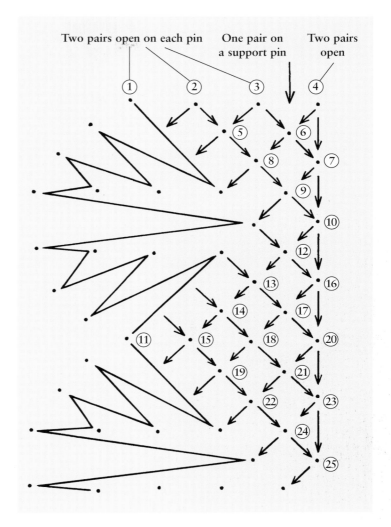

at pins **17** to **19**, and pin **20**; pins **21** to **22**, and pin **23**; and at pin **24**, and pin **25**.

11 Work the second fir tree fan, starting with the left pair hanging on pin **11** as the worker pair.**

12 Repeat from * to ** for the required length.

13 Knot each pair three times, cut off the bobbins and take out the pins.

14 To make a flower, work six repeats. Run a gathering thread along the footside edge and pull up to shape.

Fig 4.4

Boy's collar
AND EDGING

FINISHED SIZE Edging: 6 x 1in (15 x 2.5cm) and 6 x 1¾in (15 x 4.5cm)

FINISHED SIZE Collar: ¼in (7mm) wide

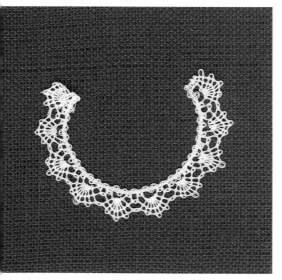

Fig 4.5

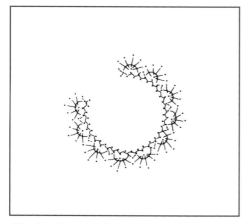

Fig 4.6 Pattern 3

*N*owadays, little boys do not wear lace collars and cuffs, but at the turn of the century it was the height of fashion. Here is a little pattern that could just as easily be used for a girl or boy.

MATERIALS

7 pairs DMC Broder Machine 50

ALTERNATIVE THREAD

Madeira Tanne 50

STITCHES USED

Double stitch ground	see page 19
French fan	see page 21
Cloth stitch trail	see page 25

METHOD

1 Hang two pairs open on pins **1** and **2**.

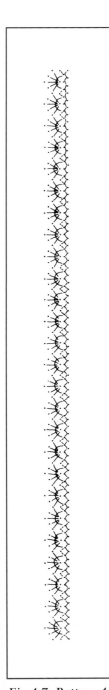

Fig 4.7 Pattern 4

2 Hang two pairs on support pins and hang to the right of the pairs from pins **1** and **2** (see Fig 4.8).

3 Hang one pair on pin **3**.

4 Twist once the pairs hanging on pin **1**. *Do not cover the pin.*

5 Twist once the pairs hanging on pin **2** and cover the pin with cloth stitch and twist.

6 With the pair at pin **3**, work to the left through three pairs in cloth stitch. Twist the worker pair and put up pin **4** under the worker pair.

7 Work to the right through three pairs in cloth stitch. Twist the worker pair and put up pin **5** under the worker pair. *Remove the support pins and pull down the spare thread.*

8 *Work to the left through two pairs in cloth stitch. Twist the worker pair and put up pin **6**.

9 Work to the right through two pairs in cloth stitch, twist the workers and put up pin **7**. Leave the workers here.

10 Twist once the fourth pair from the left.

11 Take the left pair hanging from pin **1** and work a French fan to pin **9**.

12 With the worker pair left at pin **7**, work to the left through three pairs in cloth stitch, twist the workers, remove the pivot pin **8** and re-pin under the pairs at pin **10**. Gently pull the worker pair at pin **9** and the left pair at pin **10** to flatten the loops at the base of the fan.

13 With the workers at pin **10**, work to the right through three pairs in cloth

stitch. Twist the workers and pin up at **11**.

14 Twist once the fourth pair from the left and work a cloth stitch and twist with this pair and the next pair to the left. Put up pin **12**, and cover with a cloth stitch and twist.

15 With the worker pair left at pin **11**, work to the left through three pairs in cloth stitch. Twist the workers and pin up at **13**.

16 Work to the right through three pairs in cloth stitch, twist the workers and pin up at **14**.**

17 Repeat from * to **.

18 When the lace is complete, individually knot each pair close to the pin three times. Cut off the bobbins, leaving long threads. Take the lace off the pillow and cut the ends short. Dab the cut ends with PVA glue or Fraycheck and fold under to the wrong side.

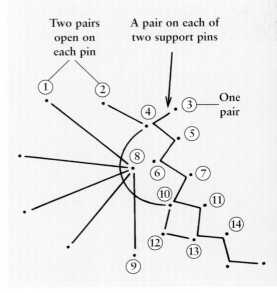

Fig 4.8

Fig 4.9

Posy Frill

FINISHED SIZE ¾in (2cm) diameter

*A*lthough this design is used as a frill for
a small posy of flowers, it could also be used
as a mat.

METHOD

WORKING CIRCULAR AND SQUARE SHAPES

This shape is worked in four sections,
turning the pillow as it is made (see Fig
4.10). Work each section with the
headside on the left and the footside on
the right (see Fig 4.11). All circular and
square shapes in this book are made in
the same way. When the fourth section is
finished, the pairs are sewn out into the
start pinholes by making a sewing.

MATERIALS

9 pairs Madeira Tanne 80

Posy of miniature flowers

Ribbon

PVA glue

ALTERNATIVE THREAD

Brok 100/2

STITCHES USED

Plait   see page 148

Picot   see page 148

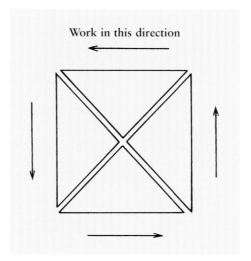

Fig 4.10

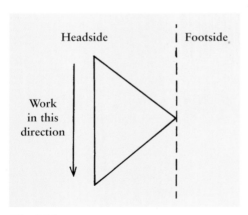

Headside | Footside

Work in this direction

Fig 4.11

1 Referring to Fig 4.12, hang eight pairs on support pins and one pair on pin **1**.

2 *The pair on pin **1** is the worker pair, which you now work to the right and left in cloth stitch, bringing in three pairs at pin **2** and one pair at each of the other pins on the right until pin **3** is put up. Remove the support pins as you work, pulling down the threads, and remember to twist the worker pair once again each time a pin is put up. Work to pin **4**.

3 With the worker pair at pin **4**, work to the left in cloth stitch through six pairs and put up pin **5**.

4 Work a plait from pin **6** to pin **7**, where a picot is made.

5 Work another plait to pin **8**.

6 With the workers left at pin **5**, continue with the cloth stitch, taking in the two pairs from the plait at pin **8**.

7 One pair is left out at pins **9** to **15**. Give each of these pairs one twist.

8 With the remaining two pairs at pin **15**, work a plait to pin **16**, where a picot is made.

9 Work another plait to pin **17**.**

10 Turn the pillow through 90° and repeat from * to **.

11 To start the next section, take the left pair of the plait as the new workers through three pairs to the right to pin **18**.

12 When the motif is complete, push down the pins into the pillow to make space to sew out the pairs in the start pinholes. Cut the threads and take out the pins.

13 Make a small bunch of flowers and put the stems through the centre hole. Secure with a little PVA glue and decorate with a bow.

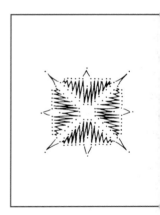

Fig 4.13
Pattern 5

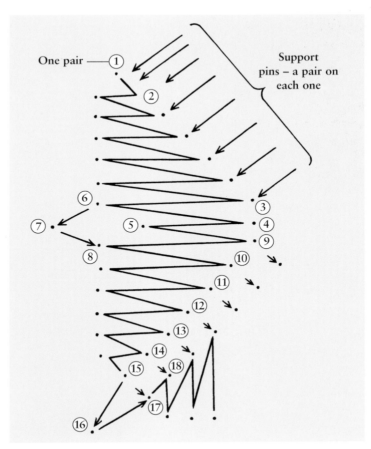

One pair — ①

Support pins – a pair on each one

Fig 4.12

Lady's
DRESS TRIMMINGS

FINISHED SIZE ⅝in (1.5cm) wide

The lady of the house is dressed in her suit, ready to take her son out to the park. Her outfit is trimmed with a small edging of Bedfordshire lace.

Fig 4.14

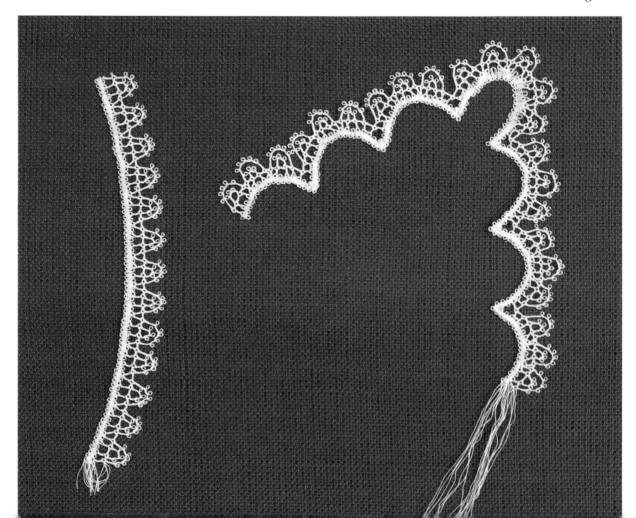

MATERIALS

9 pairs Egyptian gassed cotton 120/2

ALTERNATIVE THREAD

Brok 120/2

STITCHES USED

Cloth stitch trail	see page 25
Plait	see page 148
Picot	see page 148
Four pair crossing	see page 153

METHOD

1 Referring to Fig 4.15 hang one worker pair on pin **1** and four pairs on support pins above the work.

2 Take the worker pair to the right through these four pairs in cloth stitch, twist the workers and put up pin **2**. (Two pairs will be left out at pin **1**.)

3 Work to the left in cloth stitch through two pairs and two more pairs hanging from support pins. Twist the worker pair and put up pin **3**.

4 Work to the right in cloth stitch through four pairs, and put up pin **4**. (Two pairs are left out at pin **3**.)

5 Work to the left in cloth stitch through two pairs, twist the workers and put up pin **5**.

6 Work to the right in cloth stitch through two pairs, twist the workers and put up pin **6**.

7 There are now two pairs hanging from pins **1** and **3**. Remove the support pins and pull down the threads.

8 Work a plait from pin **1** to pin **7**.

9 Work a four pair crossing at pin **7** with the plait from pin **1** and two new pairs hanging from support pins above the work.

10 With the left two pairs, work a plait to pin **8**, where a picot is made. Remove the support pins. With the right two pairs, work a plait to pin **9**.

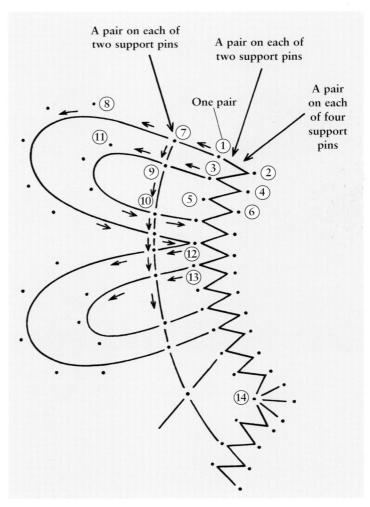

Fig 4.15

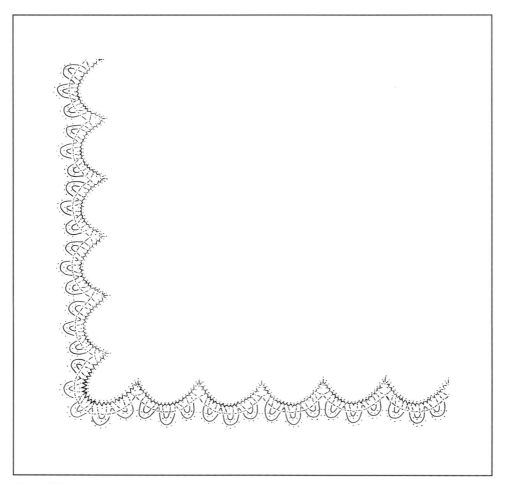

Fig 4.16 Pattern 6

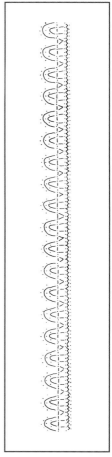

11 Work a plait with the pairs from pin **3** and then work a four pair crossing at pin **9** with the plait from pin **7**.

12 With the right two pairs at pin **9**, work a plait to pin **10**. With the left two pairs, work a plait to pin **11**, where a picot is made.

13 Continue working the pattern following Fig 4.15. At pin **12** there will be six passive pairs in the trail. Two pairs will be left out for plaits at pins **12** and **13**. Pin **14**, in the scalloped edge, will be used three times so that the trail turns the corner (back stitch, see step 2 of the edging on page 125).

Fig 4.17
Pattern 7

Small BAG

FINISHED SIZE ⅜ x ½in (10 x 3mm)

*T*here are two examples of handbags in the hall of the dolls' house. The bag next to the coatstand was made by mounting the larger roseground mat featured on page 58 onto fabric and then making this up into a bag. A chain was attached as a handle. The second bag, carried by the lady, was made with a small metal bag frame. Again, the lace was mounted onto fabric which was then made up into a bag, and the frame was attached to the top. Metallic thread was used for the handle.

MATERIALS

18 pairs Egyptian gassed cotton 170/2

Duchesse pins

Fabric

Metal handbag frame

PVA glue

Metallic thread

ALTERNATIVE THREAD

Brok 170/2

STITCHES USED

Torchon ground	see page 18
Cloth stitch diamond	see page 19
Spider	see page 22

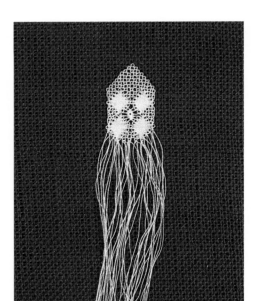

Fig 4.18

METHOD

1 Referring to Fig 4.19, hang all the pairs on support pins and work the first rows both sides in Torchon ground.

2 Continue working the pattern with the cloth stitch diamonds and spider.

3 When the lace is complete, leave it to settle on the pillow for at least 24 hours.

Fig 4.19

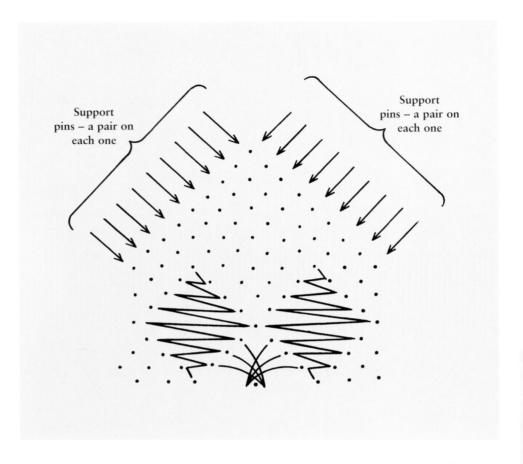

Support
pins – a pair on
each one

Support
pins – a pair on
each one

4 Take the pins out very carefully, one at a time. It is very easy to pull the fine lace out of shape.

5 When the lace is off the pillow, mount it onto fabric and make this up into a bag, concealing the cut ends at the bottom into the seam.

6 Glue the handbag frame at the top and attach metallic thread as a handle.

– TIP –

Use light, slim bobbins when working with fine threads. This will minimize thread breakages. Accurate pricking and method of working is essential when working really fine patterns.

Fig 4.20 Pattern 8

Parasol 1

FINISHED SIZE 4⁵⁄₁₆in (11cm) diameter

*A*t first glance this pattern may appear
daunting, but on closer inspection you will see
that the design is really quite simple. It will take
you a little longer to work than the earlier
patterns in this chapter, but the end result will be
well worth it.

Fig 4.21

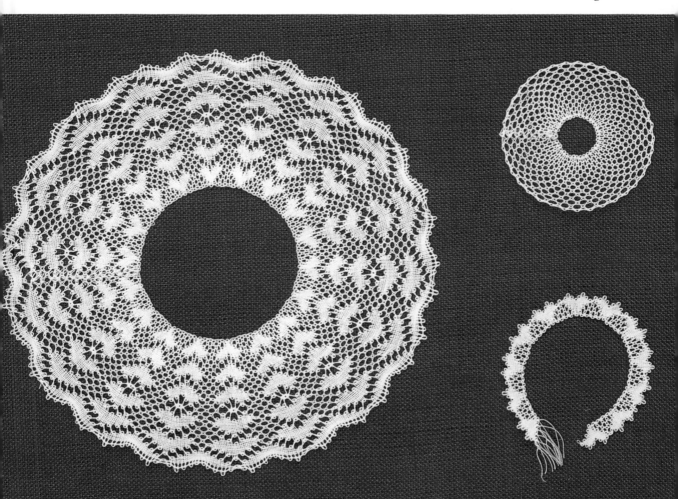

CENTRE

16 pairs Madeira Tanne 80

MAIN LACE

36 pairs Madeira Tanne 80

FRILL

7 pairs Madeira Tanne 80

Cocktail umbrella

Poster paint

PVA glue

Ribbon

Large bead

Tassel or bow

Small bead

Fabric (optional)

Fraycheck (optional)

ALTERNATIVE THREAD

Brok 100/2

STITCHES USED

Torchon ground	see page 18
Double stitch ground	see page 19
Cloth stitch shape	see page 19
Cloth stitch fan	see page 20
Spider	see page 22

METHOD

CENTRE (Fig 4.22: Pattern 9)

1 The centre circle is worked first. Put pins in on a straight line from the outer to inner edges. Hang two pairs open on each pin (see Fig 4.23).

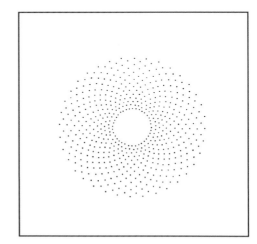

Fig 4.22
Pattern 9

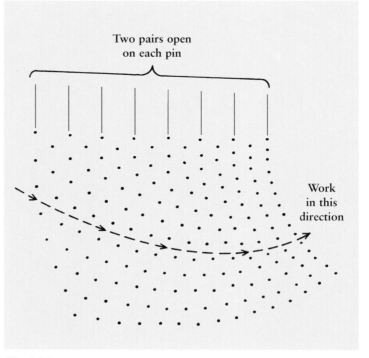

Two pairs open
on each pin

Work
in this
direction

Fig 4.23

2 The outer and inner rows of pins are worked in double stitch ground. The other pins are worked in Torchon ground. It is easier to work in curved lines from the outside inwards. *Be methodical.*

3 When the lace is complete, sew into the start pinholes. Leave the lace to settle on the pillow for 24 hours and then take it off the pillow. Take the pins out carefully.

4 Pin the main pricking (Pattern 10, Fig 4.24) onto the pillow and pin the centre lace back down, wrong side upwards, around the inner ring of pinholes on the main pricking. Put the pins in alternately every second and then third pinhole.

MAIN LACE (Fig 4.24: Pattern 10)

1 Referring to Fig 4.25, put pins in on a straight line. Hang two pairs open on each pin, twist each pair and cover with a half stitch.

2 Work the cloth stitch shapes in rows, starting from the centre. Work half of the first shape, leave, and repeat for the next shape. This gives you the pairs needed to complete the first shape.

Fig 4.24 Pattern 10

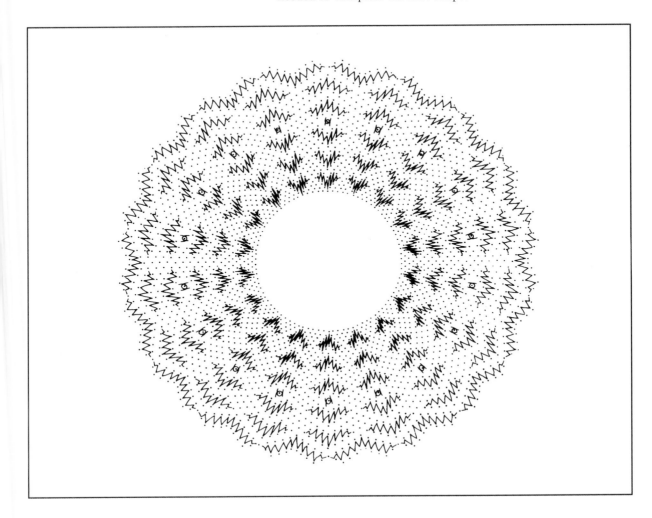

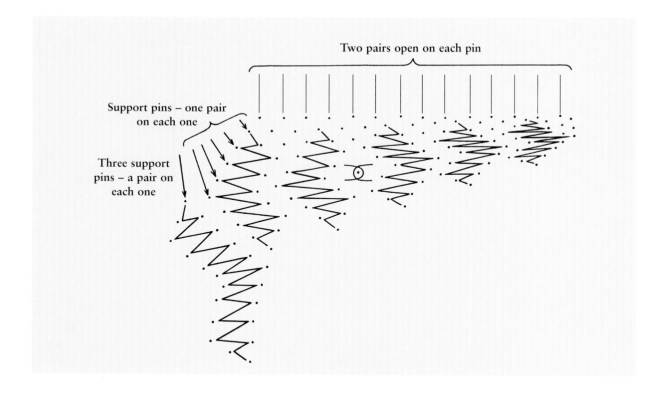

Two pairs open on each pin

Support pins – one pair
on each one

Three support
pins – a pair on
each one

Repeat this across the pattern. *Again,
be methodical.*

3 Make sewings where the centre circle
and main pattern meet, into a pinhole or
bar as appropriate. (Pairs will be sewn
in and will then go back into the main
work.)

4 When the lace is complete, sew into
the start pinholes and leave the lace to
settle for 24 hours.

FRILL (Fig 4.26: Pattern 11)
1 Referring to Fig 4.27, hang two pairs
open on pin **1** and five pairs on support
pins above the work, bringing them
down to the right of pin **1**.

2 Twist each pair hanging on pin **1**
once and cover the pin with a cloth
stitch. The right pair is the worker pair.
Now work the cloth stitch fan, bringing

in one pair from a support pin at each
pinhole on the right.

3 The ground is Torchon and the inner
row of pins is worked in double stitch
ground.

Fig 4.25

*Fig 4.26
Pattern 11*

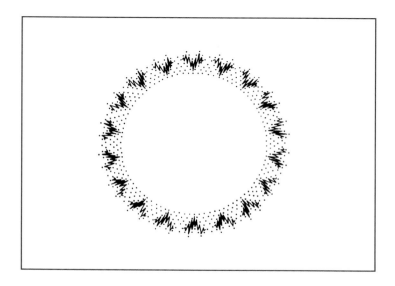

4 With the pair from pin **3** and the left pair from pin **2**, work a double stitch in pin **4**.

5 Work a Torchon ground stitch at pin **5**.

6 Start the next fan with the left pair from pin **5** as the worker pair, working to the left through two pairs in cloth stitch to put up pin **6**.

7 Work 10 repeats of the frill for the small centre hole; 27 repeats for the join of the centre circle and the main lace; and 40 repeats for the outer edge.

PREPARING THE PARASOL FRAME

1 Carefully cut off the paper from the cocktail umbrella.

2 Paint the frame with several coats of poster paint.

3 Using PVA glue, bind the parasol handle with silk ribbon and glue a large bead onto the end for a knob. Trim the handle with a tassel or bow.

MOUNTING UNLINED LACE

1 Take great care when carrying out this procedure. Using PVA glue, stick two spokes of the umbrella at a time to the lace.

2 Leave these spokes to dry before gluing the next two spokes. This ensures that the spokes are fixed firmly to the lace and do not move before the glue sets.

3 Sew the gathered frills around the small centre hole, the middle join in the lace, and the outer edge on the underside.

MOUNTING LINED LACE

1 Cut out a circle of fabric 4in (10cm) in diameter, snip out a circle in the centre 3/8in (1cm) in diameter, and then apply Fraycheck to the raw edges.

2 Sew gathered frills around the small centre hole and the middle join in the lace.

3 Stab stitch the lace onto the fabric circle around the outer edge. Glue the fabric onto the frame as described above.

4 Sew a gathered frill around the raw outer edge on the underside. Make sure that the stitches do not show on the top side.

FINISHING

Sew a small length of ribbon to the parasol lace. Work a buttonholed loop on one end of the ribbon, and sew a small bead to the other attached end. This ribbon is used to secure the parasol closed.

Fig 4.27

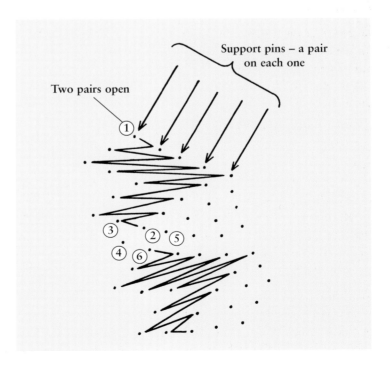

Parasol 2

FINISHED SIZE 4⁵⁄₁₆in (11cm) diameter

This parasol is constructed in the same way as Parasol 1. The use of gimp in the pattern creates a simple but effective design.

Fig 4.28

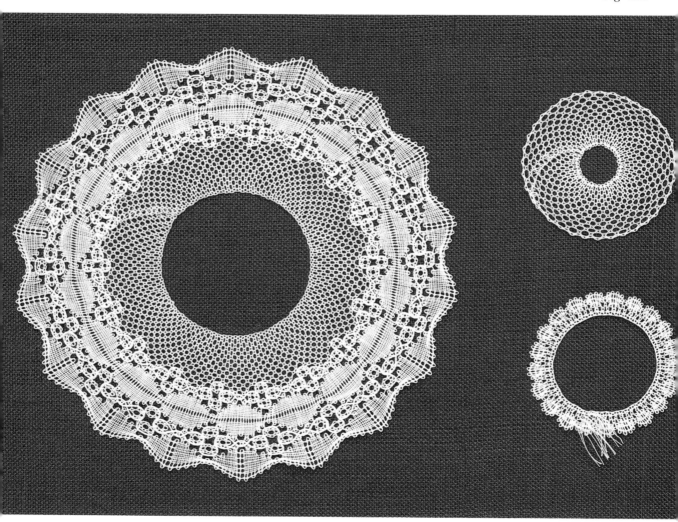

MATERIALS

CENTRE

16 pairs Madeira Tanne 80

MAIN LACE

35 pairs Madeira Tanne 80

2 pairs DMC Perle 12

FRILL

7 pairs Madeira Tanne 80

Cocktail umbrella

Poster paint

PVA glue

Ribbon

Small bead

Fabric (optional)

Fraycheck (optional)

ALTERNATIVE THREAD

Brok 100/2
DMC Flower thread

STITCHES USED

Torchon ground	see page 18
Torchon footside	see page 18
Double stitch ground	see page 19
Cloth stitch shape	see page 19
Cloth stitch fan	see page 20
Roseground 1	see page 23
Gimp thread	see page 26

METHOD

CENTRE (page 44: Pattern 9)
1 The centre circle is worked in the same way as for Parasol 1 (see page 44), but is started on a curved line. Bring in one pair at each pinhole down the line, from support pins above the work (see Fig 4.29).

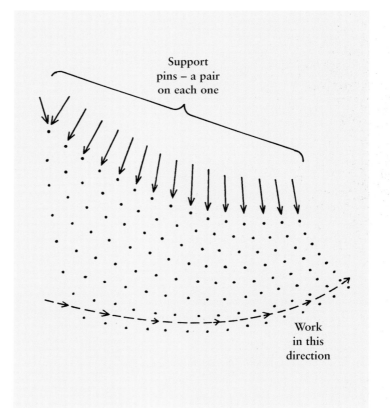

Support pins – a pair on each one

Work in this direction

Fig 4.29

Fig 4.30
Pattern 12

MAIN LACE (Fig 4.30: Pattern 12)

1 Referring to Fig 4.31, hang pairs on support pins to start the pattern.

2 Work one twist on the worker pair as it works the middle of the cloth stitch diamonds.

3 The outside edge of the fan is worked in cloth stitch and twist. In the middle of each fan, twist the passive pairs once, and then work one row in cloth stitch and twist.

4 Work the gimp around the roseground, referring to Fig 4.32.

FRILL (Fig 4.33: Pattern 13)

1 This is a simple edging. The fan is worked in cloth stitch with a cloth stitch and twist outside edge, and a cloth stitch and twist middle row (see fans in main pattern). The frill has a footside edge, and the ground is Torchon.

2 Work 17 repeats of the frill for the small centre hole; 45 repeats for the join of the centre circle and the main lace; and 78 repeats for the outer edge.

MAKING UP

Refer to the instructions for Parasol 1 for how to prepare the parasol frame and mount the lace onto it.

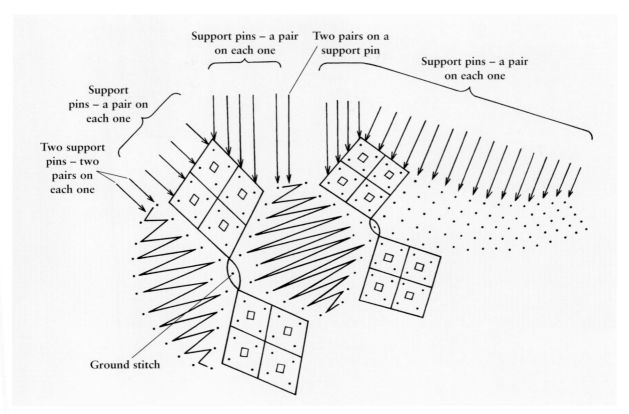

Support
pins – a pair on
each one

Two support
pins – two
pairs on
each one

Support pins – a pair
on each one

Two pairs on a
support pin

Support pins – a pair
on each one

Ground stitch

Fig 4.31

Fig 4.32

Fig 4.33 Pattern 13

The KITCHEN

Fig 5.1

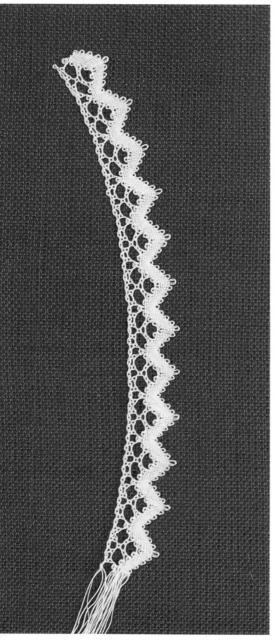

Fig 5.2

Shelf EDGING

FINISHED SIZE ⅜in (1cm) wide

*I*n *Victorian and Edwardian times, most kitchen shelves were decorated with lace. In fact, this practice was not confined just to the kitchen; the parlour mantel shelf was usually decorated in the same way.*

MATERIALS

10 pairs Madeira Tanne 80

PVA glue or Fraycheck

Gripwax

ALTERNATIVE THREAD

Brok 100/2

STITCHES USED

Cloth stitch trail	see page 25
Brabant stitch (honeycomb)	see page 159

METHOD

1 Referring to Fig 5.3, hang seven pairs on support pins above the work and one pair on pin **1**. With the pair hanging on pin **1**, work to the right in cloth stitch

54

through the seven pairs which are hanging from support pins. Twist the worker pair and put up pin **2**.

2 Work to the left in cloth stitch through seven pairs, twist the worker pair and put up pin **3**. *Remove the support pins and pull down the spare thread.*

3 *Continue working the cloth stitch trail, leaving out one pair at pins **2**, **4**, **5** and **6**. Twist each of these pairs twice.

4 Leave the worker pair uncovered at pin **7**. There are three passive pairs in the trail at this point.

5 Hang two pairs open on pin **8**, twist each pair once and cover the pin with a cloth stitch and twist.

6 The pinholes to the right of the trail are worked in Brabant stitch, with cloth stitch and twist on the outside edge.

Referring to Fig 5.3, work in number order. Pins **9**, **11**, **13**, **14**, **15**, **17** and **18** are worked in half stitch, pin, half stitch and twist. Pins **10**, **12**, **16** and **19** are worked in cloth stitch and twist, pin, cloth stitch and twist (double stitch).

7 Return to the worker pair left at pin **7** and continue working the cloth stitch trail, bringing in one pair at pinholes **20** to **23**.**

8 Repeat from * to ** for the required length.

9 When the lace is complete, take it off the pillow, cut the ends short and dab with PVA glue or Fraycheck. Fold the ends back to the wrong side.

10 To secure the lace edging to the shelf, apply Gripwax at each end and lightly press the lace onto the shelf.

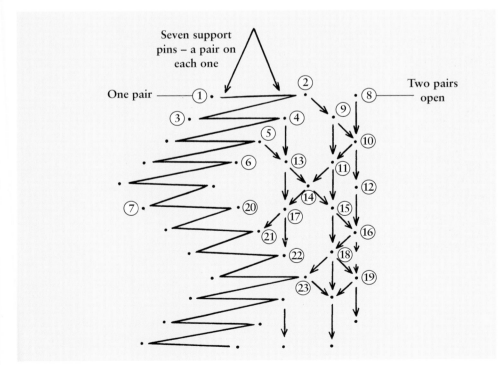

Fig 5.3

Fig 5.4
Pattern 14

Fig 5.5

Jug COVER

FINISHED SIZE 1¼in (3cm) diameter

This little mat has a variety of uses. Here in the kitchen it is used as a beaded cover for a jug, but it can also be used as a pretty mat or sewn onto a cushion, as seen in the lacemaker's cottage on page ii.

MATERIALS

8 pairs DMC Broder Machine 50

1 single gimp bobbin DMC Perle 12

18 small beads (make sure your crochet hook will fit through)

Crochet hook

Fraycheck

ALTERNATIVE THREAD

Madeira Tanne 80
DMC Flower thread

STITCHES USED

Double stitch ground	see page 19
French fan	see page 21
Cloth stitch trail	see page 25

METHOD

1 Referring to Fig 5.6, hang two pairs open on pin **1**, twist each pair and cover the pin with a cloth stitch and twist. Repeat for pin **2**.

2 Hang a single gimp bobbin from a support pin.

3 With the right pair hanging from pin **1** as workers, work a French fan, working through the gimp thread and then through the left pair from pin **2**, putting up pivot pin **4**. Work back through one passive pair, through the gimp, and through the edge pair to put up the outside edge pin. Continue working the French fan.

4 When the middle edge pin of the fan has been put up, add a bead. Put a crochet hook through the bead and hook one of the worker threads through the bead. Put the other worker bobbin through the loop made and pull up the

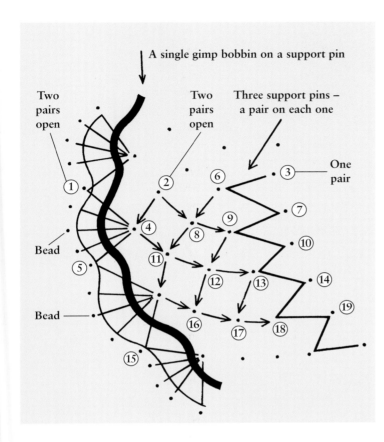

A single gimp bobbin on a support pin

Two pairs open

Two pairs open

Three support pins – a pair on each one

One pair

Bead

Bead

Fig 5.6

threads to the pin. Twist the workers twice to hold the bead in place.

5 When the fan is complete, leave the workers at pin **5** uncovered.

6 With the pair hanging at pin **3**, work to the left in cloth stitch through the three pairs which are hanging from support pins. Twist the workers and put up pin **6**.

7 Work to the right through three pairs in cloth stitch and put up pin **7**. Twist the left pair at pin **6**.

8 With the right pair from pin **2** and the pair from pin **6**, work double stitch ground at pin **8**.

9 Take the workers at pin **7** to the left through three pairs (two passive pairs and the right pair from pin **8**) in cloth stitch.

– TIP –

To make the jug cover hang realistically, spray the lace lightly with clean water, place it over the jug and cover both with cling film. Pull down the film and twist it under the jug. Leave to dry naturally and then remove the film.

Put up pin **9** and then work back to the right through three pairs in cloth stitch. Put up pin **10**. *Remove the support pins and pull down the spare thread.*

10 *Take the pair hanging from pivot pin **4** and the left pair from pin **8** and work double stitch ground in pin **11**. Remove pivot pin **4** and gently pull on the fan workers to flatten the loops made around the pin.

11 Work pin **12** in double stitch ground. Bring the workers through the cloth stitch trail from pin **10** and put up pin **13**. Return to pin **14** in cloth stitch.

12 With the workers left at pin **5**, work the next French fan to pin **15**. Remember to add a bead at the middle pin.

13 Work pins **16** and **17** in double stitch ground. Work pins **18** and **19** as for pins **13** and **14**.***

14 Repeat from * to ** until all the pinholes are worked, turning the pillow gradually as you work.

15 Sew out the pairs into the start pinholes. Cut the gimp threads close to the lace, take the lace off the pillow, and dab with a little Fraycheck to secure.

Fig 5.7 Pattern 15

Roseground MATS

FINISHED SIZE ¾in (2cm) and 1in (2.5cm) diameter

*T*wo *roseground mats are shown here in the kitchen. The large version was used to decorate the handbag on page 31.*

There are a variety of ways in which these mats can be worked. Different interpretations for the same patterns could use cloth stitch or half stitch fans with either roseground, spider, Torchon ground or cloth stitch squares in the centre. You will also be able to think up your own variations.

Fig 5.8

LARGE MAT

11 pairs Madeira Tanne 80

SMALL MAT

9 pairs Madeira Tanne 80

ALTERNATIVE THREAD

Brok 100/2

STITCHES USED

Torchon ground	see page 18
Cloth stitch fan	see page 20
Roseground 1	see page 23

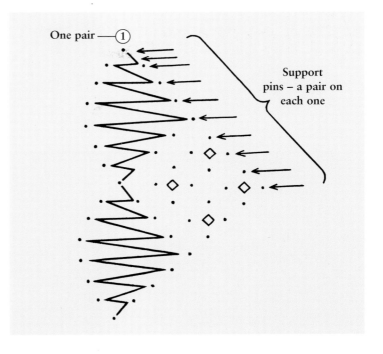

*Fig 5.10
Diagram for
Pattern 17.*

METHOD

1 These mats are worked in sections, following the instructions for Working Circular and Square Shapes on page 36.

2 Referring to Figs 5.9 and 5.10, hang pairs from support pins.

3 Work the fan first and then work the roseground section. *Remember to remove the support pins and pull down the spare thread.* Make sure each pair has a twist and then turn the pillow through 90° and work the next section, starting with a fan.

4 Sew out the pairs into the start pinholes.

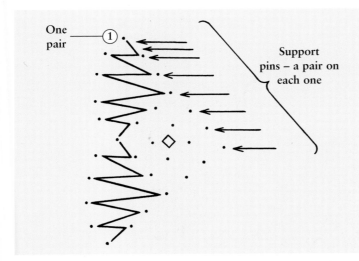

Fig 5.9

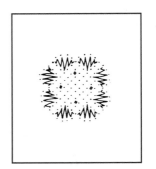

*Fig 5.11
Pattern 16*

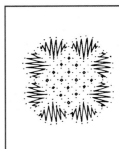

*Fig 5.12
Pattern 17*

Small TRAY CLOTH

FINISHED SIZE 1 x 1⅜in (2.5 x 3.5cm)

Fig 5.13

*T*he cook is busy preparing food for the day's meals. The tray, with its tray cloth, is waiting to be loaded with refreshments for the family upstairs.

METHOD

1 Referring to Fig 5.14, work the top two fans first, in the direction shown.

2 Hang two pairs open on pin **1**, twist each pair once and cover the pin with a cloth stitch. The right pair will be the workers for the top two fans. The left pair will be the workers for the fans on the left side of the tray cloth.

3 Hang four pairs open on a glass-headed support pin above the work. Secure the pairs by twisting the threads around this pin and pushing it right into the pillow. The two pairs on the right will be the passive pairs for the top two fans. The two pairs on the left will be the passive pairs for the fans on the left side of the tray cloth.

4 With the right pair hanging from pin **1**, work to the right in cloth stitch through the right two passive pairs on the glass-headed support pin. Put up pin **2**.

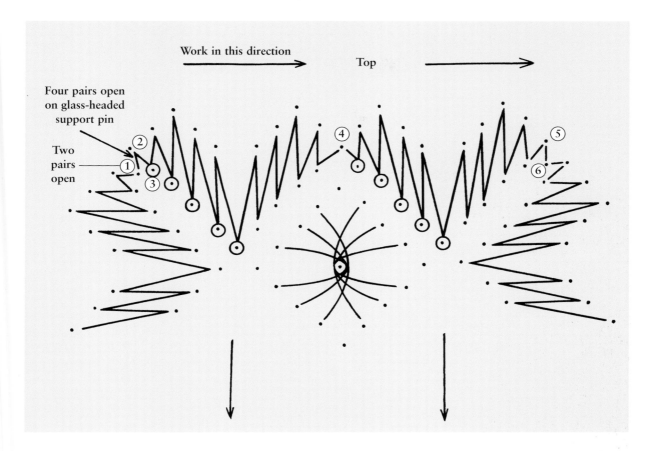

Work in this direction

Top

Four pairs open
on glass-headed
support pin

Two
pairs
open

Fig 5.14

5 Work back to the left through two pairs in cloth stitch. Hang two pairs open on a support pin to the left of pin **1** and continue the workers through the first of these two pairs in cloth stitch. Put up pin **3**.

6 Put the left pair from the support pin behind a divider pin. This will be worked later.

7 Continue working the first fan in cloth stitch, hanging two pairs open on support pins on the left and bringing in the first of these pairs at the circled holes on the left side. Each time, put the other pair hanging on the support pin behind the divider pin to be worked later. As you work down, remember to remove the support pins.

8 When you reach the widest point of the fan, leave out a pair at each pin on the left as the fan reduces in size until, at pin **4**, there will be two passive pairs and one worker pair.

9 Repeat for the second fan, bringing in one pair at the circled pins and leaving one pair behind the divider pin, to be worked later.

10 When pin **5** is put up, turn the pillow through 90°. The pattern can now be worked downwards. Remove the glass-headed support pin before working the first fan on the left.

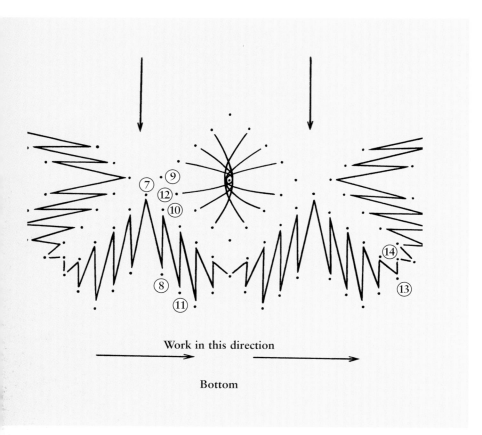

Work in this direction

Bottom

Fig 5.15

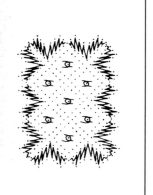

Fig 5.16
Pattern 18

each pin and tie off; repeat for the other two bobbins). Remember to twist each pair before tying off.

16 Take the workers in cloth stitch to the right and left again, putting up pins **10** and **11**. Tie and lay back the two pairs at pins **10** and **12** as before.

17 Complete the first fan in this way. Try to keep the passive pairs in the fan to the right, to make the work neat.

18 Repeat for the second fan, finishing at pin **13**. There should be two worker pairs and four passive pairs.

19 Take the two worker pairs through the passive pairs and work them together. Pin up at **14**. Cover the pin with cloth stitch.

20 Turn the pillow through 90° and tie off the remaining pairs over the work. Take one bobbin from each side, starting with the middle two bobbins. Working in this way ensures that the thread ends are taken back over the work and will not show when the work is taken off the pillow.

21 When each pair has been tied off, bunch the middle bobbins together, cross the two outside pairs underneath the bunch, and again tie these two outside pairs over the bundle.

22 Cut off the bobbins, leaving long ends. Take the lace off the pillow and cut the threads close to the work.

11 Follow Fig 5.14 carefully, making sure that the first fans at either side are started in the correct direction. Do not miss pin **6**.

12 Work down to the bottom of the pattern, starting with the top spider, until the final two fans remain to be worked.

13 Push down as many pins as possible flat into the pillows.

14 Turn the pillow through 90° and work the last two fans in the direction shown in Fig 5.15.

15 Work the first half of the fan to pin **8**. Now tie off the pairs from pin **7** and pin **9** individually and lay them back over the work (take one bobbin from

Cake FRILL

FINISHED SIZE ⁵⁄₁₆in (8mm) wide

*T*his pattern could also be used for a frill
down the front bodice of a blouse or dress.
In the bedroom (see page 104) the young
lady has a garter which has been made
from the same pattern.

MATERIALS

14 pairs Egyptian gassed cotton 170/2

Duchesse pins

Ribbon

Cake

ALTERNATIVE THREAD

Brok 170/2

STITCHES USED

Torchon ground	see page 18
Half stitch trail	see page 25

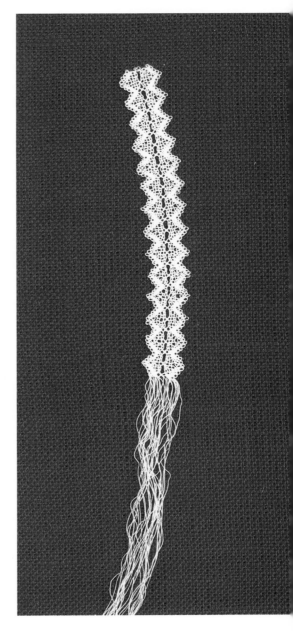

Fig 5.17

Fig 5.18

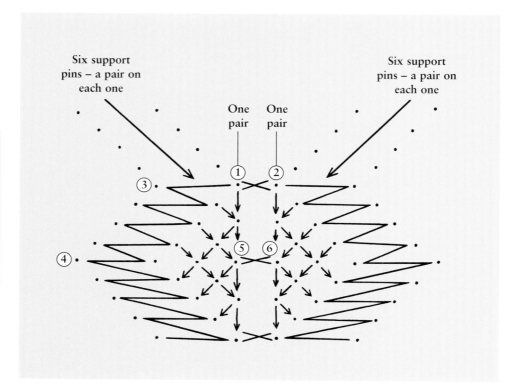

Six support
pins – a pair on
each one

Six support
pins – a pair on
each one

One
pair

One
pair

METHOD

1 Referring to Fig 5.18, hang one pair on pin **1** and one pair on pin **2**. Work a cloth stitch and twist with these two pairs. These two pairs are the workers, which now work the outside half stitch trails.

2 Take the left pair to the left through six pairs, which are hung from support pins, in half stitch, and put up pin **3**. Work the trail to pin **4**, leaving out pairs on the right side. Remember to take out the support pins before you work too far.

3 Repeat for the other side.

4 Work the Torchon ground on either side.

5 At pins **5** and **6**, work half stitch and put up pins. Work the inner two pairs together in cloth stitch and twist. Cover pins **5** and **6** with half stitch.

6 When the Torchon ground is complete, return to the trails and continue.

7 When the lace is complete, leave it to settle on the pillow for at least 24 hours. Take the pins out very carefully. It is very easy to pull the lace out of shape.

8 Take the lace off the pillow and thread ribbon through the middle. Place the frill around the cake and add a bow over the join, to cover the ends of the threads.

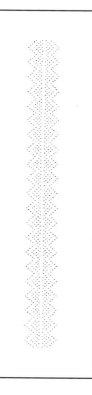

*Fig 5.19
Pattern 19*

Café CURTAIN

FINISHED SIZE 1½in (4cm) deep

*T*his café curtain is shown hanging from halfway down the window. It could also be hung from the top of the window for a different effect.

Fig 5.20

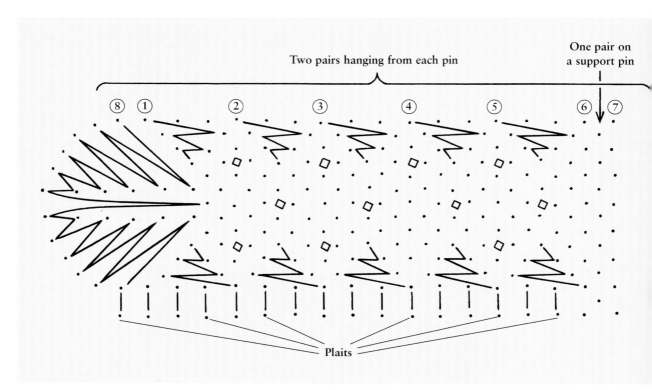

Two pairs hanging from each pin

One pair on a support pin

⑧ ① ② ③ ④ ⑤ ⑥ ⑦

Plaits

Fig 5.21

MATERIALS

37 pairs Madeira Tanne 80

PVA glue or Fraycheck

Milliner's elastic (thin)

ALTERNATIVE THREAD

Brok 100/2

STITCHES USED

Torchon ground	see page 18
Torchon footside	see page 18
Cloth stitch triangle	see page 19
Fir tree fan	see page 21
Roseground 1	see page 23
Plait	see page 148

— TIP —

Pull up the elastic to the width of the window so that the lace is gathered. Pin out the folds onto an ironing board and spray the lace with clean water. Leave to dry naturally in folds. This gives the curtain a realistic look as it hangs at the window.

METHOD

1 Referring to Fig 5.21, put a pin in each of the top row of holes and hang two pairs open on each. Hang one pair on a support pin above the work and bring the pair down where shown.

BECOME A REGULAR SUBSCRIBER TO

The Dolls' House Magazine

TODAY, AND YOU WILL ENJOY...

The Secrets of the Dolls' House Makers
Jean Nisbett

NEVER MISSING AN ISSUE!
Priority delivery – never miss an issue.

SATISFACTION GUARANTEED!
Guaranteed enjoyment – if you are not 100% satisfied let us know and we will refund the balance of your subscription.

SPECIAL DISCOUNT!
An incredible 20% DISCOUNT on all one-year subscriptions.

FREE BOOK When you take a 2-year subscription.
Receive free, Jean Nisbett's comprehensive book, 'The Secrets of the Dolls' House Makers', retail price £16.95 ($21.95).

20% DISCOUNT ~ FREE BOOK

	UK £	US $	OVERSEAS £
12 MONTHS • 10 ISSUES	~~35.95~~ 28.75	~~69.95~~ 55.95	~~42.50~~ 34.00
24 MONTHS • 20 ISSUES	65.00	129.95	75.00
BEST BUY • 2-year subscription includes FREE BOOK! • BEST BUY			

Please send my copies of *The Dolls' House Magazine* to:

Mr/Mrs/Ms ....

Address ....

....

Postcode .... Tel ....

I wish to start my subscription with the month/issue (please complete)

....

CREDIT CARD HOTLINE TEL: 01273 488005 OR FAX 01273 478606

I enclose a cheque to the total value of ☐ £/$

made payable to GMC Publications Ltd.

OR Please debit my credit card* to the value of ☐ £/$

☐ VISA ☐ AMERICAN EXPRESS ☐ ●●● ☐ MasterCard ☐ SWITCH *please indicate   Switch issue number ☐☐

Account No. ☐☐☐☐☐☐☐☐☐☐☐☐☐☐☐☐☐☐

Expiry Date ☐☐☐☐   Signature _____

Please post your order to:

Guild of Master Craftsman Publications
Castle Place, 166 High Street, Lewes, East Sussex BN7 1XU England

2 At pins **1**, **2**, **3**, **4** and **5**, twist each pair once and cover the pin with a cloth stitch. Twist the left pair on each pin once.

3 At pin **6**, twist each pair once and cover the pin with a half stitch.

4 At pins **7** and **8**, twist each pair once and cover the pin with a cloth stitch and twist.

5 Twist all other pairs once and leave the pins uncovered.

6 Complete the cloth stitch triangles, fir tree fan, roseground centre and Torchon footside in the first section.

7 At the bottom of the section, put up pins. Work plaits and put up pins along the top of the next section.

8 When the lace is complete, take it off the pillow, cut the ends short and dab with PVA glue or Fraycheck. Fold back to the wrong side.

9 Thread some thin milliner's elastic through the footside edge and hang halfway down your window on small hooks placed on either side of the window frame.

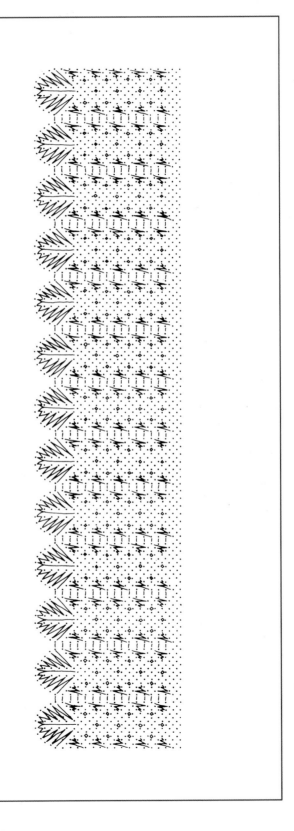

Fig 5.22 Pattern 20

The
DINING
ROOM

Fig 6.1

Table mat
EDGINGS

FINISHED SIZE ¾ x ⅜ x ⅜in (2 x 1 x 1cm) and 1½ x ¾ x ¾in (4 x 2 x 2cm)

*T*hese little triangular shapes are very versatile. They can be used in any combination of numbers to edge mats or tablecloths. Shown in the dining room is a mat edged with three triangular shapes. Four around a square mat would look good, or you could finish a tablecloth with a row of shapes around the edge.

Fig 6.2

MATERIALS

SMALL MAT

11 pairs Madeira Tanne 80

LARGE MAT

17 pairs Madeira Tanne 80

Fine cotton lawn

ALTERNATIVE THREAD

Brok 100/2

STITCHES USED

SMALL MAT

Half stitch diamond	see page 19
Cloth stitch fan	see page 20
Cloth stitch trail	see page 25

LARGE MAT

Spider	see page 22
Cloth stitch trail	see page 25
Half stitch shape	see page 25

METHOD

SMALL MAT (Fig 6.4: Pattern 21)

1 Referring to Fig 6.3, hang one pair on pin **1** and three pairs side by side on a support pin above the work.

2 Take the worker pair on pin **1** left through the three pairs on the support pin in cloth stitch, twist the workers, and put up pin **2**. Work back to the right through three pairs in cloth stitch, twist the workers, and put up pin **3**.

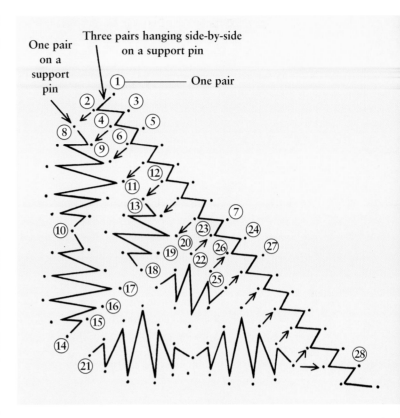

Fig 6.3

3 Push the left pair at pin **2** away to the left of the pillow and put a divider pin in front to prevent the pair from moving. This pair will be used later.

4 Put a support pin above the work and hang one pair on it. Take the workers at pin **3** to the left in cloth stitch through the two passive pairs and then through the pair hanging on the support pin. Twist the worker pair and put up pin **4**.

5 *Work back to the right through three pairs in cloth stitch, twist the worker pair and put up pin **5**.

6 Push the left pair at pin **4** to the left out of the way and put it behind the divider pin to be used later.

7 Hang another pair on a support pin above the work and take the worker pair at pin **5** through the passive pairs and the

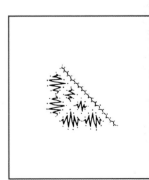

Fig 6.4
Pattern 21

pair from the support pin in cloth stitch, twist the worker pair and put up pin **6**.**

8 Repeat from * to **, adding one pair at each of the next four pins on the left until pin **7** is put up. Twist all the pairs hanging from the left pins once.

9 Now work the fan. Remove the divider pin and hang one pair on a support pin above the work. Work a cloth stitch with this pair and the pair hanging from pin **2**, and put up pin **8**. *Remove the support pins and pull down the spare thread.*

10 With the worker pair on the left, work to the right through two pairs in cloth stitch, twist the worker pair and put up pin **9**. Continue working the fan until pin **10** is put up.

11 Start the half stitch diamond at pin **13** with the pairs from pins **11** and **12**.

12 When the diamond is complete, work the second fan, finishing at pin **14**. Leave the pin uncovered.

13 Turn the pillow through 90° and twist each pair hanging from pins **15** to **20**.

14 Work a cloth stitch with the two pairs hanging at pin **14** and put pin **21** between them. Work the next fan. (Note that the worker pair has changed.)

15 Next, work the second half stitch diamond, and then the last fan. All the pairs from the work now have to be taken into the cloth stitch trail on the right, and they will gradually be thrown to the back of the work.

16 With the worker pair at pin **7**, work to the left in cloth stitch through the two passive pairs and the pair hanging from

pin **22**. Twist the worker pair and put up pin **23**.

17 Work to the right through three pairs in cloth stitch, twist the worker pair and put up pin **24**.

18 Number the passive bobbins in the trail from right to left, 1 to 6. Take number 2 and 4 bobbins and lay them back over the work at 180° to the pins.

19 *Take the worker pair at pin **24** to the left in cloth stitch through the two passive pairs and the pair hanging from pin **25**. Twist the worker pair and put up pin **26**.

20 Work to the right through three pairs in cloth stitch, twist the worker pair and put up pin **27**.

21 Lay back number 2 and 4 bobbins from the trail as before.**

22 Repeat from * to ** until pin **28** is put up. There are three pairs left.

23 Finish the cloth stitch trail. Tie each pair three times and then cut off all the bobbins, leaving long ends.

24 Remove the pins and take the lace off the pillow. Cut the threads close to the lace, taking care not to cut into your work.

25 Fold back the tab of cloth stitch to the wrong side and stitch carefully to secure.

26 Attach the lace to the fabric with small stitches and cut away the excess fabric (see page 162).

LARGE MAT (Fig 6.5: Pattern 22)
The large triangle is started and finished in a similar way to the small triangle. Work the lace following the pattern.

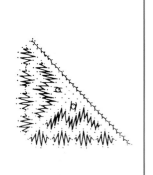

Fig 6.5
Pattern 22

Table napkin
EDGING

*T*his very tiny pattern only has five pairs
of bobbins and is quick to work. It would
also look very nice frilled around a small
photograph frame.

MATERIALS

5 pairs Egyptian gassed cotton 170/2

Fine cotton lawn

ALTERNATIVE THREAD

Brok 170/2

STITCHES USED

Torchon ground	see page 18
Plait	see page 148
Picot	see page 148

Fig 6.6

Fig 6.7

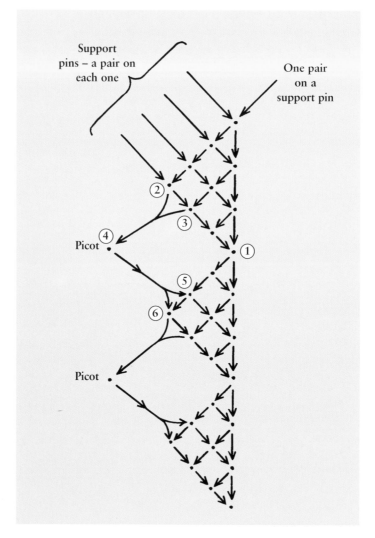

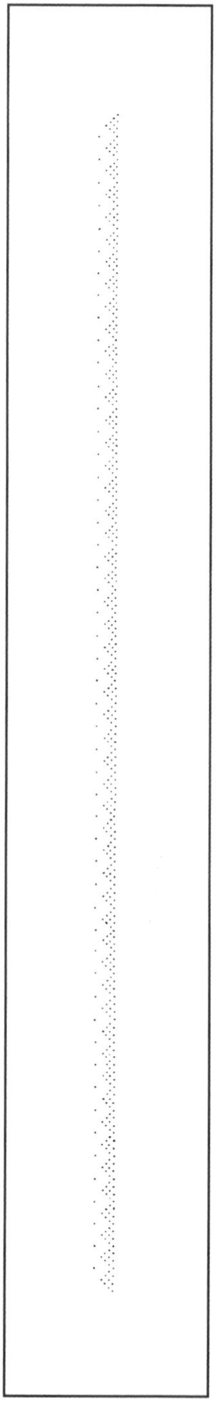

METHOD

1 Hang five pairs on support pins above the work and, following Fig 6.7, work the Torchon ground, finishing at pin **1**. *Remember to remove the support pins and pull down the spare thread.*

2 *With the pairs from pins **2** and **3**, work a plait to pin **4**, where a picot is made. (Make three twists before the picot pin and two twists after.)

3 Work the next area of Torchon ground, taking in the two plait pairs at pins **5** and **6**.**

4 Repeat from * to ** for the required length.

5 Stitch the edging onto a small piece of cotton lawn. Fold the napkin and lay it on the table ready for lunch.

Fig 6.8
Pattern 23

Tablecloth EDGING

A *combination of different stitches can be worked on this edging. The example in the photograph shows two different fans and two triangles on the footside edge, so you can choose which combination you like best. I have worked cloth stitch triangles, with cloth stitch fans on the tablecloth edging.*

MATERIALS

13 pairs Madeira Tanne 80

Fine cotton lawn

ALTERNATIVE THREAD

Brok 100/2

STITCHES USED

Torchon ground	see page 18
Cloth stitch and half stitch shapes	see page 19
Cloth stitch and half stitch fans with double stitch edge	see page 20
Spider	see page 22

Fig 6.9

METHOD

Measure the top of your table. Add 1½in (4cm) around this measurement for the overhang and mark with pins. Add another ⅝in (1.5cm) to the measurements and cut out the fabric to this size. Measure the length marked by pins. Add approximately 4in (10cm) to this measurement to give the amount of lace to be worked.

1 Referring to Fig 6.10, hang two pairs open on pin **1**, twist each pair and cover the pin with double stitch. The right pair is the worker pair for the fan. Hang 10 pairs on support pins above the work.

2 With the worker pair on pin **1**, work through two pairs to the right in cloth stitch and put up pin **2**.

3 Hang one worker pair on pin **3** and work to the left through two pairs in cloth stitch. Put up pin **4**.

4 Following Fig 6.10, take pairs into the work from the support pins.

5 Work the required length. Sew out into the start pinholes.

6 Pin the lace around the edge of the fabric, with the wrong side of the lace to the right side of the fabric. Place the edge of the fans against the edge of the fabric, and tack the lace and fabric together close to the footside edge. If making a square tablecloth, gather the lace slightly around the corners. If making a circular tablecloth, gather the lace slightly all the way around the edge. Sew the lace to the fabric through the footside holes (see page 162) and then cut away the excess fabric at the back, taking care not to cut into the lace. Neaten the raw edge with small blanket stitches.

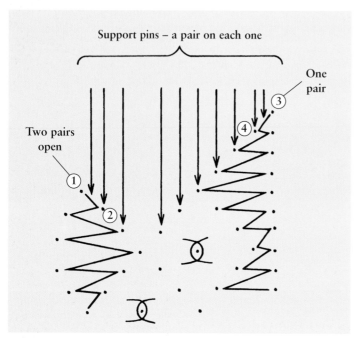

Fig 6.10

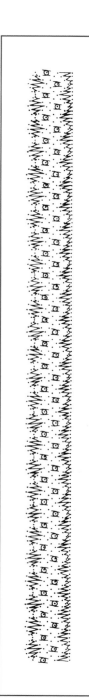

Fig 6.11
Pattern 24

– TIP –

To make the tablecloth hang realistically, cover the table with cling film and place the cloth centrally over the top. Spray the cloth with clean water and cover with another layer of cling film. Pull the film down to create folds in the tablecloth and leave to dry naturally before removing the film.

Large
TRAY CLOTH

FINISHED SIZE 1¼ x 1¾in (3 x 4.5cm)

*T*he lady of the house would be proud to serve her guests tea from a tray covered with this pretty tray cloth. It is started and finished in the same way as the small tray cloth on page 60.

MATERIALS

30 pairs Madeira Tanne 80

ALTERNATIVE THREAD

Brok 100/2

STITCHES USED

Torchon ground	see page 18
Cloth or half stitch diamond	see page 19
Cloth stitch fan	see page 20
Spider	see page 22

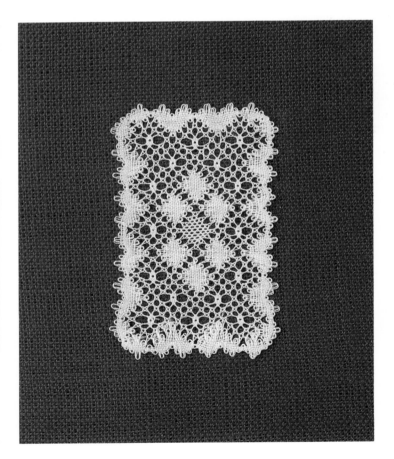

Fig 6.12

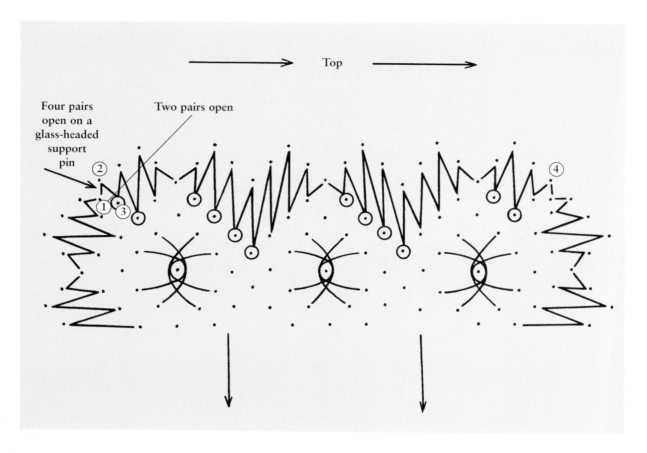

Top

Four pairs
open on a
glass-headed
support
pin

Two pairs open

② ① ③ ④

Fig 6.13

METHOD

1 Refer to Fig 6.13, and also to Figs 5.14 and 5.15 and the instructions on page 60 for the small tray cloth. Bring in two pairs on each circled hole until at pin **4** all 30 pairs are in the work.

2 The lace is finished in the same way as the small tray cloth (see page 62). This pattern can be extended to make a table runner (see page 97).

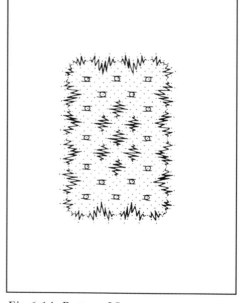

Fig 6.14 Pattern 25

Large
SQUARE MAT

FINISHED SIZE 1⅞ x 1⅞in (4.8 x 4.8cm)

*T*his mat is shown hanging over the edge of a side table. It would look just as nice placed in the middle of the dining table, or even as a wrap for the baby in the nursery.

MATERIALS

22 pairs Madeira Tanne 80

ALTERNATIVE THREAD

Brok 100/2

STITCHES USED

Torchon ground	see page 18
Cloth stitch diamond	see page 19
Cloth stitch fan with double stitch edge	see page 20
Spider	see page 22
Roseground 1	see page 23

Fig 6.15

Fig 6.16

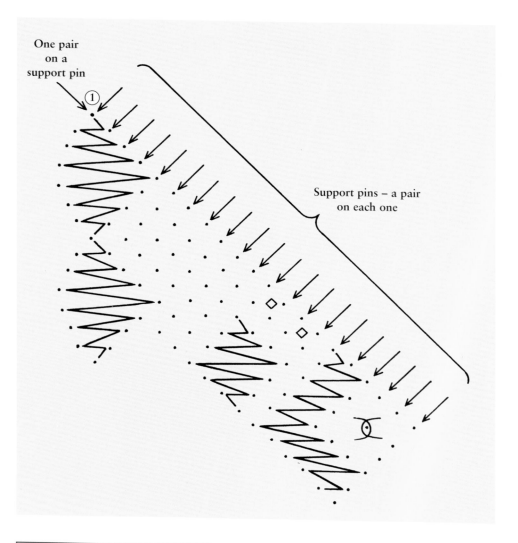

One pair
on a
support pin

①

Support pins – a pair
on each one

Fig 6.17
Pattern 26

Method

1 Work pin **1** in double stitch with two pairs from support pins.

2 Hang all the other pairs on support pins and then bring them into the work, following Fig 6.16.

3 Work down the mat until the first section is finished. Following the instructions for Working Circular and Square Shapes on page 36, turn the work through 90° and continue with the second and then subsequent sections.

Curtains

FINISHED SIZE 2⅞ x 4⅝in (7.3 x 11.8cm)

Windows always look charming when they are hung with lace curtains. Do not be daunted by the size of the patterns, because the method of work is really quite simple.

MATERIALS

78 pairs Madeira Tanne 80

PVA glue or Fraycheck

Milliner's elastic (thin)

ALTERNATIVE THREAD

Brok 100/2

STITCHES USED

Torchon ground	see page 18
Torchon footside	see page 18
Cloth stitch diamond	see page 19
Cloth stitch fan with double stitch edge	see page 20

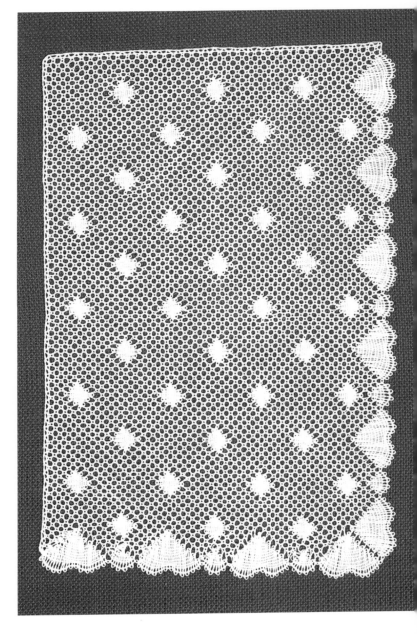

Fig 6.18

METHOD

A large number of bobbins are needed to work this pattern, so careful management is needed to complete it successfully. Group the bobbins onto stitch-holders and stack them to one side when not in use.

LEFT CURTAIN – HEADSIDE ON LEFT (Fig 6.21: Pattern 27)

1 Referring to Fig 6.19, start at the top left. Hang four pairs open on pin **1**. Work a double stitch with the left two pairs, and twist the other two pairs.

2 *Put up pin **2** under the right pair hanging on pin **1**, and hang two pairs open on it (see Fig 6.20).

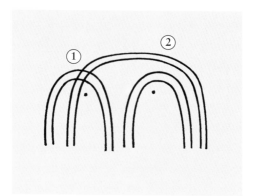

Fig 6.20

3 Twist the left pair hanging on pin **2** and cloth stitch and twist the right two pairs.**

4 Repeat from * to ** in all the pinholes along the top row.

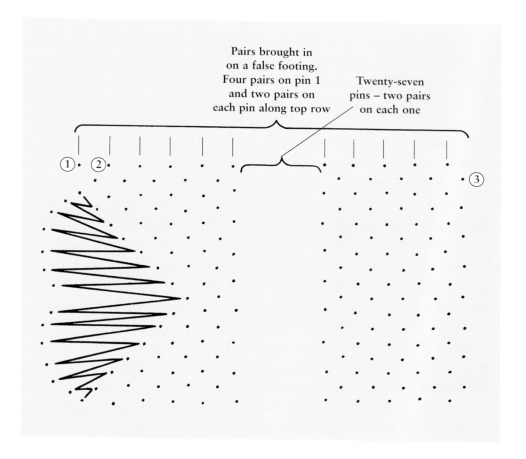

Pairs brought in on a false footing. Four pairs on pin 1 and two pairs on each pin along top row

Twenty-seven pins – two pairs on each one

Fig 6.19

5 With the second pair from the left, work to the right through all the pairs in cloth stitch and twist.

6 At pin 3 on the right side, pin up under two pairs and cover the pin with cloth stitch and twist (this gives a footside edge along the top and down the right side).

7 Work down the pattern until the bottom rows of fans are left to work. Turn the pillow through 90° and finish as for the small tray cloth on page 62.

> **– TIP –**
>
> *To make sure that the ground works evenly when working large areas, always work the rows in the same direction.*

RIGHT CURTAIN – HEADSIDE ON RIGHT (Fig 6.22: Pattern 28)

Reverse the instructions to work the right curtain.

HANGING

1 To lengthen or shorten the curtains, add or take away pattern repeats between the lines on the patterns (see pages 161 and 162).

2 Prepare the curtains for hanging as for the café curtains on page 66.

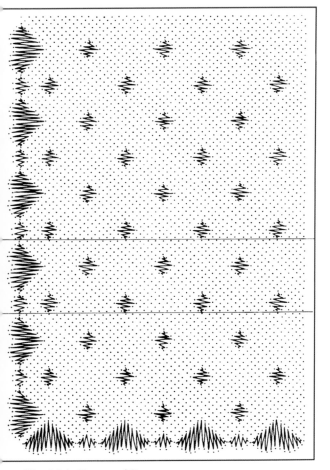

Fig 6.21 Pattern 27

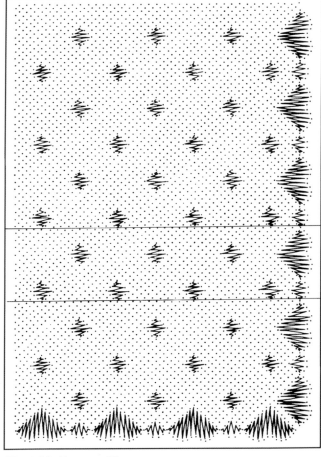

Fig 6.22 Pattern 28

CHAPTER SEVEN

The
PARLOUR

Fig 7.1

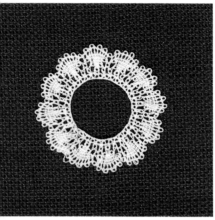

Fig 7.2

Cushion MOTIF

FINISHED SIZE ¹⁵⁄₁₆in (2.4cm) in diameter

Mounted onto a small piece of linen, this circular edging would also be the perfect finish for a little mat.

MATERIALS

7 pairs Madeira Tanne 80

Cushion

ALTERNATIVE THREAD

Brok 100/2

STITCHES USED

Torchon ground	see page 18
Torchon footside	see page 18
Cloth stitch fan with double stitch edge	see page 20

METHOD

1 Referring to Fig 7.3, hang seven pairs on support pins above the work.

2 Work a cloth stitch and twist with two pairs on the left and put up pin **1**. Cover the pin with a cloth stitch and twist.

3 The right pair hanging on pin **1** is the worker pair. *Work to the right through one pair in cloth stitch. Put up pin **2**.

4 Work to the left through one pair in cloth stitch, twist the workers and then work the next pair on the left in cloth stitch and twist. Put up pin **3**.

5 Work to the right through one pair in cloth stitch and twist, and two pairs in cloth stitch. Put up pin **4**.

6 Work to the left through two pairs in cloth stitch, twist the workers and then work the next pair on the left in cloth stitch and twist. Put up pin **5**.

7 Work to the right through one pair in cloth stitch and twist, and three pairs in cloth stitch. Put up pin **6**. *Remove the support pins and pull down the spare thread.*

8 Work to the left through three pairs in cloth stitch, twist the workers, and then work the next pair on the left in cloth stitch and twist. Put up pin **7**.

9 Work to the right through one pair in cloth stitch and twist, and two pairs in cloth stitch. Put up pin **8**.

10 Work to the left through two pairs in cloth stitch, twist the workers, and then work the next pair on the left in cloth stitch and twist. Put up pin **9**.

11 Work to the right through one pair in cloth stitch and twist, and one pair in cloth stitch. Put up pin **10**.

12 Work to the left through one pair in cloth stitch, twist the workers, and then work the next pair on the left in cloth stitch and twist. Put up pin **11** and cover the pin.

13 Take the pair hanging from pin **6** through the remaining two pairs hanging from support pins in cloth stitch and twist.

14 Put up pin **12** under two pairs. (Under two pairs means to the left of the two pairs just worked.) (Footside edge.)

15 Cover pin **12** with cloth stitch and twist with the two pairs on either side of the pin.

16 Work Torchon ground stitch at pin **13** with the pair from pin **8** and the left pair from pin **12**.

17 Work Torchon ground stitch at pin **14** with the pair from pin **10** and the left pair from pin **13**.

18 Work footside edge at pin **15** by taking the right pair from pin **13** through two pairs to the right in cloth stitch and twist. Pin up under two pairs and cover with a cloth stitch and twist.

19 Work Torchon ground stitch at pin **16** with the right pair from pin **14** and the left pair from pin **15**.

20 Work footside edge at pin **17** following step 18.**

21 Start the next fan with the right pair hanging on pin **11** as the workers. Repeat from * to **.

22 When you reach the beginning of the circle, sew out into the start pinholes.

23 Sew the lace circle onto a cushion of your choice.

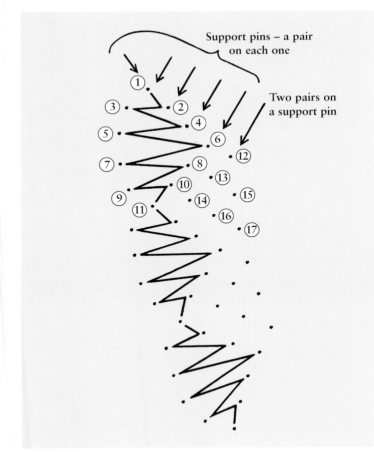

Fig 7.3

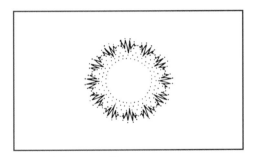

Fig 7.4 Pattern 29

Chair BRAID

FINISHED SIZE ⅛ x ⁵⁄₃₂in (3 x 4mm) wide

*T*his little braid can be used in many different ways. As well as for upholstery, it could also be used to trim coats, hats and dresses in the Victorian and Edwardian styles.

MATERIALS

TWISTED CORD

PATTERN 30, FIG 7.9 7 pairs Madeira Tanne 80

1 pair DMC Flower thread

PATTERN 31, FIG 7.10 5 pairs Madeira Tanne 80

1 pair DMC Flower thread

CHAIN

PATTERN 30, FIG 7.9 5 pairs Madeira Tanne 80

2 pairs DMC Flower thread

PATTERN 31, FIG 7.10 3 pairs Madeira Tanne 80

2 pairs DMC Flower thread

ALTERNATIVE THREADS

Brok 100/2

DMC Perle 12

Fig 7.5

STITCHES USED

Cloth stitch	see page 13

METHOD

TWISTED CORD

1 Hang the worker pair on the top left pin and the other pairs on support pins above the work. Hang the thicker pair in the middle of these pairs (see Fig 7.6).

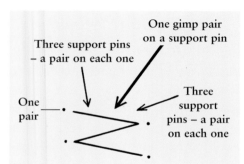

One pair

Three support pins – a pair on each one

One gimp pair on a support pin

Three support pins – a pair on each one

Fig 7.6

2 Take the workers in cloth stitch through half of the thin passive pairs to the middle of the braid.

3 Take both the worker threads over the first thick thread and under the second. Twist the thick threads right over left (see Fig 7.7).

4 Take the workers in cloth stitch to the end of the row and put up the top right pin.

5 Work back to the left in cloth stitch. Take both the worker threads under the first thick thread and over the second. Twist the thick threads right over left.

6 Complete the row in cloth stitch and pin up on the left. Continue in this way

for the required length, remembering to *remove the support pins and pull down the spare thread.*

CHAIN

This is similar to twisted cord but it is worked with four thick threads. Note that each pair of thick threads is crossed (left over right) on the left, and twisted (right over left) on the right (see Fig 7.8).

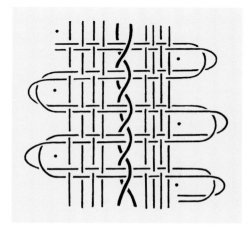

Fig 7.7

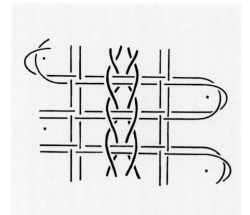

Fig 7.8

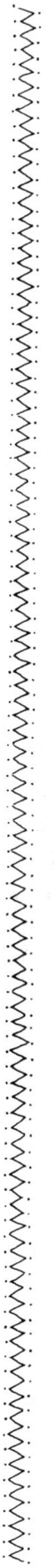

Fig 7.9 RIGHT Pattern 30

Fig 7.10 FAR RIGHT Pattern 31

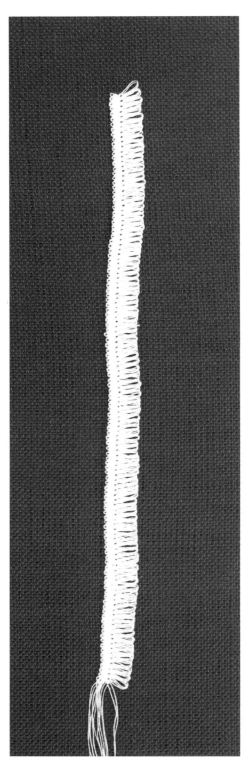

Fig 7.11

Chair FRINGE

FINISHED SIZE ⁹⁄₃₂in (7mm) wide

*T*his pattern is quite slow to work, but if you persevere the results are very worthwhile.

As an alternative, make the fringe in a different colour to the braid, and for extra interest add to the braid a twisted cord or chain (see page 88) in the fringe colour.

MATERIALS

6 pairs Madeira Tanne 80

Duchesse pins

ALTERNATIVE THREAD

Brok 100/2

STITCHES USED

Cloth stitch   see page 13

METHOD

1 Referring to Fig 7.12, hang three pairs on support pins above the work. Hang one worker pair on pin **1**.

2 Hang two pairs on pin **2**. (These are fringe pairs and can be in a contrasting colour.)

3 *Take the pair on pin **1** through all the pairs to the left in cloth stitch.

4 Put up pin **3** under the workers. Work a cloth stitch with the two fringe pairs.

5 Work back through all the pairs to the right in cloth stitch and put up pin **4**. *Remove the support pins and pull down the spare thread.*

6 Put up pin **5** under the fringe pair (i.e. take the fringe pairs anticlockwise around the pin at **5**).**

7 Repeat from * to ** for required length.

8 The fringe can be left looped or it can be cut.

> **– TIP –**
>
> *To make the fringe longer, extend the left side pins further from the braid.*

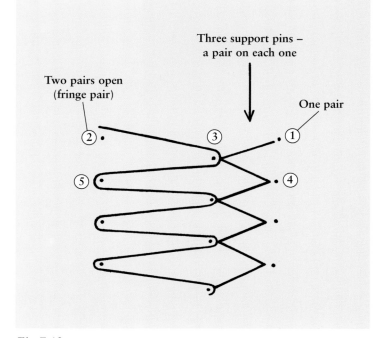

Fig 7.12

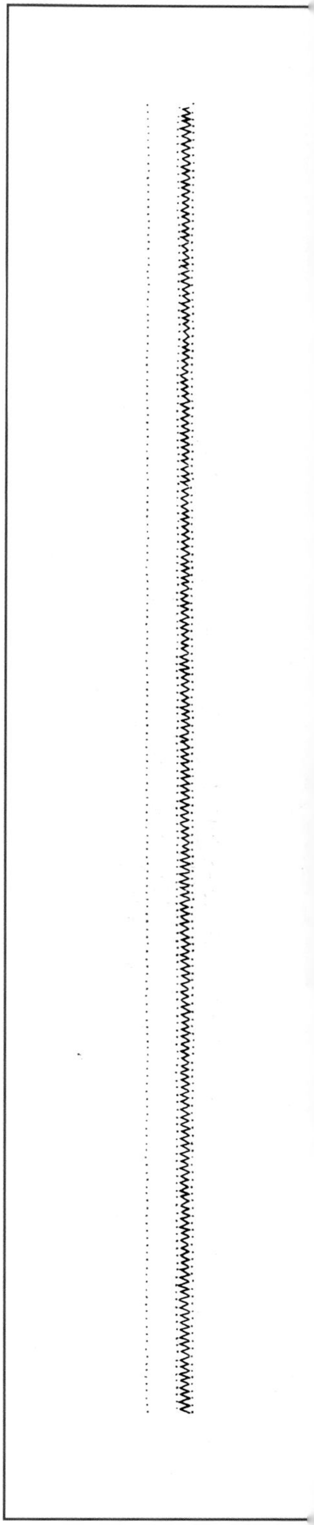

Fig 7.13
Pattern 32

Bookmark

FINISHED SIZE ½ x ⁵⁄₃₂in (13 x 4mm)

Fig 7.14

MATERIALS

8 pairs Egyptian gassed cotton 170/2

Duchesse pins

Ribbon ⅛in (3.5mm) wide

PVA glue

ALTERNATIVE THREAD

Brok 170/2

STITCHES USED

Torchon ground	see page 18
Spider	see page 22

A small but easy pattern to work. Be very careful when you have finished and are taking out the pins. It is easy to pull the lace out of shape.

METHOD

1 Hang all the pairs on support pins above the work and bring into the pattern following Fig 7.15. Once the work is established, remember to *remove the support pins and pull down the spare thread.*

2 This is a very simple pattern, but care must be taken not to miss pinholes. Work the pattern until the last two diagonal rows of pinholes are left.

3 Work pins **1** and **2** in Torchon ground (see Fig 7.16).

4 Work the pair from pin **3** through two pairs to the left in cloth stitch and pin up at **4**. Cover with cloth stitch.

5 Take the left pair at pin **5** through three pairs to the left in cloth stitch and pin up at pin **6**. Cover with cloth stitch. Throw out the fourth pair from the left to the back of the work.

6 Reversing the instructions, work the other side to pin **7**. Six pairs are left.

7 Work the three pairs on the left through the three pairs on the right in cloth stitch and put up pin **8** (this is the first half of the spider's body).

8 Keep the outside pairs on the left and right to the sides and bunch the other four pairs together in your left hand.

9 Cross the outside two pairs under the bunch and lay the bunch down onto the pillow.

10 Take one bobbin from either side and knot over the bunch. Repeat with the other two bobbins.

11 Cut the threads long to form a tassel. Cut the thrown-out threads close to the work.

12 Leave the lace to settle on the pillow for 24 hours and then take the pins out very carefully.

13 Glue the lace onto a short length of ribbon to make a bookmark.

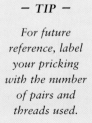

– *TIP* –

For future reference, label your pricking with the number of pairs and threads used.

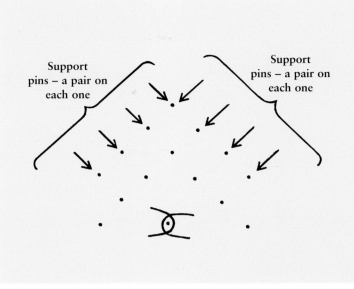

Fig 7.15

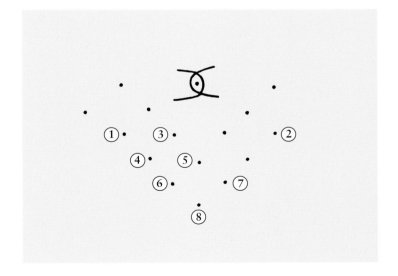

Fig 7.16

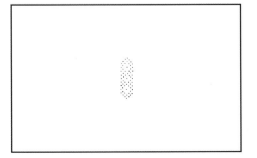

Fig 7.17
Pattern 33

Antimacassar AND CHAIR ARM COVERS

FINISHED SIZE Main pattern: ¾ x 1¹⁵⁄₃₂in (2 x 3.7cm)

FINISHED SIZE Edging: ⁷⁄₃₂in (5mm) wide

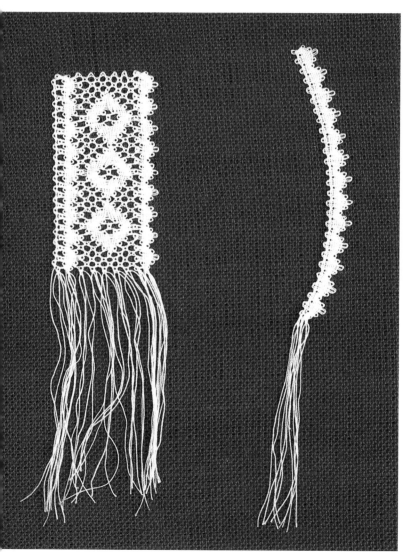

G*entlemen used to use macassar oil on their hair, so antimacassars were put on the backs of arm chairs to protect the fabric.*

MATERIALS

MAIN LACE

20 pairs Madeira Tanne 80

EDGING

5 pairs Madeira Tanne 80

Fine cotton fabric

ALTERNATIVE THREAD

Brok 100/2

Fig 7.18

STITCHES USED

Torchon ground	see page 18
Cloth stitch diamond with hole	see page 158

METHOD

MAIN LACE (Pattern 34, Fig 7.21)

1 Referring to Fig 7.19, hang one pair on pin **1** and four pairs on support pins above the work. Take the pair on pin **1** through four pairs to the right in cloth stitch. Pin up at **2**.

2 Work back to the left in cloth stitch and put up pin **3**.

3 Hang two pairs open on pins **4** to **8**, give each pair a twist and cover the pins with half stitch.

4 Hang one pair on pin **9**. Hang three pairs on support pins above the work. Take the pair on pin **9** through three pairs to the right in cloth stitch. Pin up at **10**.

5 Work back to the left through four pairs in cloth stitch and put up pin **11**.

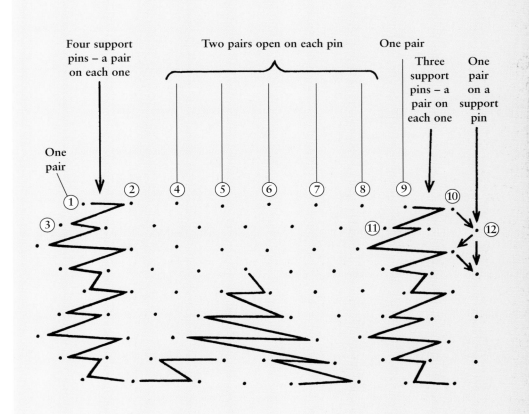

Fig 7.19

6 Hang a pair on a support pin above the work. Work a cloth stitch and twist with this pair and the right pair from pin **10** and put up pin **12**. Cover the pin with a cloth stitch and twist.

7 Continue with the pattern as now set.

EDGING (Fig 7.22: Pattern 35)

1 Referring to Fig 7.20, hang the worker pair on pin **1** and four pairs on support pins above the work.

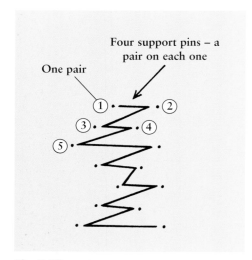

Fig 7.20

2 Take the workers through the four pairs in cloth stitch and put up pin **2**.

3 *Work to the left through four pairs in cloth stitch and put up pin **3**.

4 Work to the right through three pairs in cloth stitch and put up pin **4**.

5 Work to the left through three pairs in cloth stitch and put up pin **5**.

6 Twist the extreme right pair once.**

7 Repeat from * to **.

8 Work three pieces of lace each 2in (5.2cm) long.

MAKING UP THE ANTIMACASSAR

1 Cut a piece of fabric 2¼in (6cm) square.

2 Sew the main lace to one short end of the fabric. Sew the other edgings onto the other sides.

3 Trim the fabric, being careful not to cut the lace, and neaten the fabric edges.

CHAIR ARM COVERS

1 Cut two pieces of fabric to fit your chair arms.

2 For each piece, work two lengths of lace to sew onto opposite sides of the arm cover. Hem the other two sides.

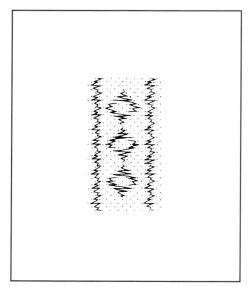

Fig 7.21
Pattern 34

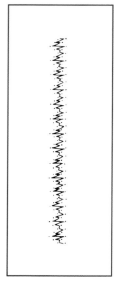

Fig 7.22
Pattern 35

Table RUNNER

FINISHED SIZE 1³⁄₁₆ x 2³⁄₄ or 3²¹⁄₃₂ or 4²¹⁄₃₂in (3 x 7 or 9.3 or 11.8cm)

*T*his table runner is an adaptation of the large tray cloth on page 77. Patterns are given for three different lengths, so that the runner can lie flat on the table top or hang over the edge of the sideboard, as in the parlour and the lacemaker's cottage (see page ii).

MATERIALS

30 pairs Madeira Tanne 80

ALTERNATIVE THREAD

Brok 100/2

Fig 7.23

STITCHES USED

Torchon ground	see page 18
Half stitch or cloth stitch diamond	see page 19
Cloth stitch fan	see page 20
Spider	see page 22

METHOD

1 Follow the instructions for the large tray cloth (see page 77) and for the small tray cloth (see page 60).

Fig 7.24 Pattern 36   *Fig 7.25 Pattern 37*   *Fig 7.26 Pattern 38*

Bell PULL

FINISHED SIZE 2¾ x ⁵⁄₁₆in (7cm x 8mm)

*B*ell pulls were a necessity in well-to-do Victorian and Edwardian homes for summoning servants from 'below stairs' to serve afternoon tea or to fetch the master's pipe and slippers. This little design looks effective mounted on some ribbon with a brass bell at the bottom.

MATERIALS

15 pairs Egyptian gassed cotton 120/2

Grosgrain ribbon ³⁄₈in (1cm) wide

Brass bell

Brass jump ring

ALTERNATIVE THREAD

Brok 120/2

STITCHES USED

Torchon footside	see page 18
Plait	see page 148
Leaf	see page 151
Six pair crossing	see page 153

Fig 7.27

METHOD

1 Referring to Fig 7.28, hang four pairs open on pin **1**. Twist the two pairs on the left of the pin, and work cloth stitch and twist with the other two pairs.

2 The inner pairs are the workers. Let the pair on the left hang to the back of the pillow and secure it with a glass-headed pin.

3 Hang four pairs open (passives for both directions) around pin **2** and, using the workers to the left of pin **1**, work in cloth stitch through the two pairs to the right of pin **2**. Now work through the same two pairs of passives with the workers to the right of pin **1**. Twist these workers and put up pin **3**.

Fig 7.29
Pattern 39

4 Work back in cloth stitch and work a Torchon footside at pin **4**. Continue to pin **5**.

5 Turn the pillow through 180° and remove pin **2**. Put in pin **6** between the worker and passive pairs.

6 Work to the footside at pin **7**, remove the glass-headed pin securing the edge pair and work the footside pin at **7**.

7 Continue working to **2** and add two pairs here for the leaf. Turn the pillow through 180°, so that the curved edge is again at the top of the pillow. Also add two pairs at pins **5** and **8**.

8 Work leaves from pins **2**, **5** and **8** and a six pair crossing in the centre at pin **9**.

9 Work three more leaves to reach pins **10**, **11** and **12**. Work two plaits to reach pin **12**, where another six pair crossing is worked. Work the next section in half stitch.

10 When the lace is complete, cut a piece of ribbon 6¼in (16cm) long. Sew the lace to the ribbon near one end, leaving enough ribbon to turn under. Fold the rest of the ribbon back under the lace, turn in the ends and stitch around the edge, enclosing the ends of the threads in the seam. Attach a bell at the rounded end and a jump ring at the other.

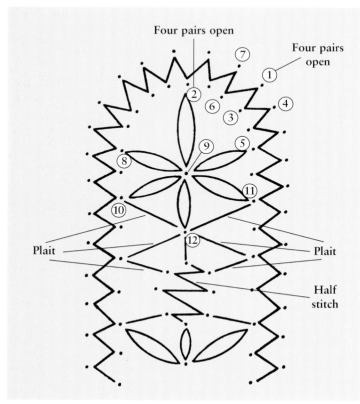

Fig 7.28

Patchwork TABLECLOTH

FINISHED SIZE 4¾ x 4¾in (12 x 12cm)

*T*his is an ambitious project, but you will learn
many new stitches in the process. It will take a
few weeks to complete the tablecloth.

Fig 7.30

MATERIALS

58 pairs Madeira Tanne 80

1 pair DMC Perle 12

ALTERNATIVE THREAD

Brok 100/2

DMC Flower thread

METHOD

Each square has 7 x 7 pinholes (the lines on the pricking are for guidance only). Some squares have extra lines of Torchon ground to complete the shape. Referring to Fig 7.31, work stitches as follows, in number order.

1 Cloth stitch square with Torchon ground surround (see page 19).

2 Roseground 3 (Torchon ground top row left and right) (see page 154).

3 Bias ground 1 (Torchon ground bottom row left and right) (see page 155).

4 Spider with five legs each side (see page 22).

5 Zig-zag of cloth stitch in Torchon ground (see page 25).

6 Twisted hole ground (see page 159).

7 Roseground 2 (Torchon ground top row left and right) (see page 154).

8 Gimp in Torchon ground (see page 26).

9 Roseground 1 (Torchon ground bottom row left and right) (see page 23).

10 Cloth stitch square with twists on the workers and passives (see page 19).

11 Woven stitch (see page 160).

12 Compound spiders (see page 156).

13 Triangular ground (Torchon ground rows top right and bottom right) (see page 160).

14 Small cloth squares, pairs twisted four times between each square (Torchon ground top rows left and right) (see page 19).

15 Roseground 4 (Torchon ground top rows left and right) (see page 155).

16 Raised leaf on cloth stitch square (see page 152).

17 Half stitch square with Torchon ground surround (see page 19).

18 Leaves with six pair crossing (see page 153).

> **– TIP –**
>
> *Be organized in your work. Use stitch-holders for each set of seven pairs.*

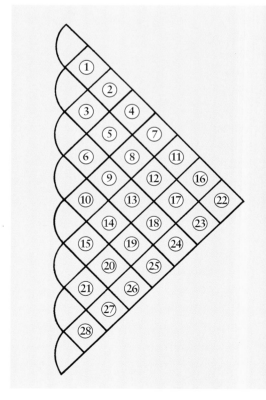

Fig 7.31

19 Round spider (Torchon ground bottom rows left and right) (see page 157).

20 Torchon mayflower (see page 159).

21 Torchon ground (see page 18).

22 Cloth stitch shape and spider (see pages 19 and 22).

23 Bias ground 2 (Torchon ground bottom rows left and right) (see page 155).

24 Brabant (honeycomb) (see page 159).

25 Square tallies in Torchon ground (see page 152).

26 Cane ground (Torchon ground bottom rows left and right) (see page 160).

27 Roseground 5 (Torchon ground rows top left and bottom right) (see page 155).

28 Cloth stitch square with small hole and a Torchon ground surround (see page 158).

The fans are worked in cloth stitch, with cloth stitch and twist on the outside edge pair. The worker pair is twisted two pairs in from the outside edge.

Fig 7.32
Pattern 40

Fig 8.1

Bedlinen
EDGING

FINISHED SIZE ⁷⁄₃₂in (5mm) wide

A small, simple edging that will
have many uses in your dolls' house.

MATERIALS

7 pairs Egyptian gassed cotton 120/2

Fine cotton lawn

Embroidery thread (optional)

Ribbon bows (optional)

ALTERNATIVE THREAD

Brok 120/2

STITCHES USED

Double stitch ground   see page 19

Cloth stitch trail   see page 25

Fig 8.2

METHOD

WORKING THE LACE

1 Referring to Fig 8.3, hang two pairs open on pin **1**. Twist each pair and cover the pin with cloth stitch and twist.

2 Hang four pairs on support pins above the work. Hang one worker pair on pin **2**.

3 Take the workers at pin **2** to the right through the four pairs on support pins in cloth stitch, through the left pair on pin **1** in cloth stitch and put up pin **3** under the worker pair.

4 *Take the workers to the left through five pairs in cloth stitch and put up pin **4**.

5 Take the workers to the right through four pairs in cloth stitch and put up pin **5**. *Remove the support pins and pull down the spare thread.*

6 Take the workers to the left through four pairs in cloth stitch and put up pin **6**.

7 Take the workers to the right through three pairs in cloth stitch and put up pin **7**.

8 Take the workers to the left through three pairs in cloth stitch and put up pin **8**. Leave the pin uncovered.

9 Work a cloth stitch and twist with the pair from pin **3** and the pair from pin **1**, and put up pin **9**. Cover the pin with a cloth stitch and twist.

10 Work cloth stitch and twist with the pair from pin **5** and the left pair from pin **9**. Put up pin **10** and cover with cloth stitch and twist.

11 Work cloth stitch and twist with the pair from pin **9** and the right pair from pin **10**. Put up pin **11** and cover with cloth stitch and twist.

12 Return to the workers on the left at pin **8** and continue the cloth stitch trail. Work to the right through four pairs in cloth stitch and put up pin **12**.

13 Work to the left through four pairs in cloth stitch and put up pin **13**.

14 Work to the right through five pairs in cloth stitch and put up pin **14**.**

15 Repeat from * to ** for the required length.

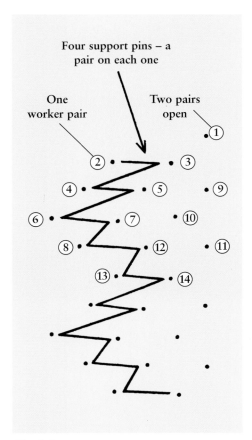

Four support pins – a
pair on each one

One
worker pair

Two pairs
open

Fig 8.3

MAKING UP THE PILLOWCASE

1 Cut a piece of fabric measuring 6 x 2³⁄₈in (15 x 6cm). Hem both short ends. Sew a length of lace onto one short end.

2 Following Figs 8.4 and 8.5, and with the right sides together, fold A–A to B–B. Fold C–C over the top and seam both long sides. Turn right side out.

3 If desired, finish off the pillowcase with embroidery and ribbon bows.

MAKING UP THE TOP SHEET

1 Cut a piece of fabric measuring 9¼ x 7in (23.5 x 18cm) for a single bed, 9¼ x 8½in (23.5 x 21.5cm) for a double bed.

2 Hem both long sides and one short side, taking a ³⁄₈in (1cm) allowance.

3 Hem the remaining width on the wrong side, taking a ⁵⁄₈in (1.5cm) allowance. (Hemming on the wrong side means that when the top of the sheet is turned over, the lace shows on the right side.) Decorate with lace.

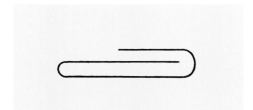

Fig 8.5

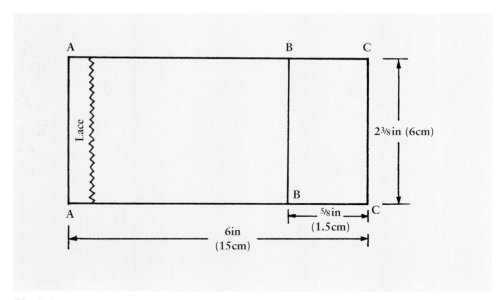

Fig 8.4

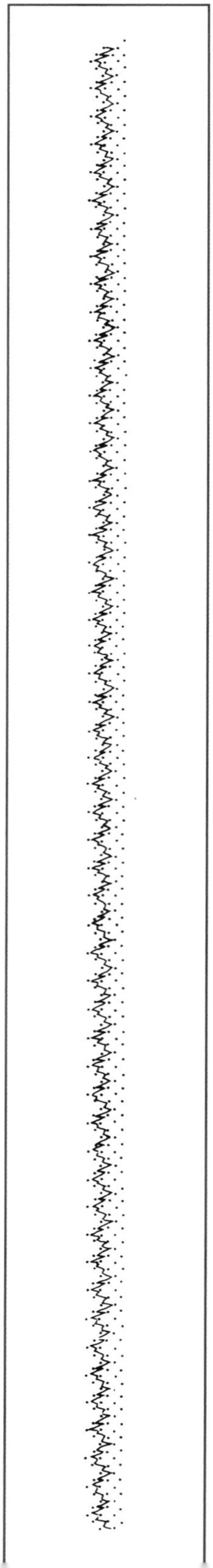

Fig 8.6
Pattern 41

Underwear
EDGING

FINISHED SIZE ¼in (6mm) wide

*T*his edging is very versatile and could be used to edge a curtain as well as the underwear (petticoat, drawers and basque) shown on pages 104 and 105. The lacemaker in her cottage (see page ii) has some of the edging on a card ready for the dealer to buy.

MATERIALS

6 pairs DMC Broder Machine 50

ALTERNATIVE THREAD

Madeira Tanne 50

STITCHES USED

Double stitch ground	see page 19
French fan	see page 21

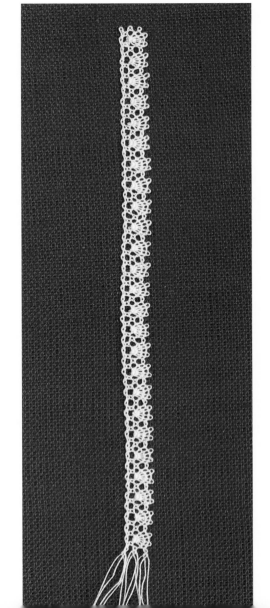

Fig 8.7

METHOD

1 Referring to Fig 8.8, hang two pairs open on pins **1**, **2** and **3**. Give each pair a twist and cover each pin with a cloth stitch and twist.

2 Work double stitch ground at pin **4** with the right pair hanging at pin **2** and the left pair hanging at pin **1**.

3 Work double stitch ground at pin **5** with the pair hanging from pin **1** and the right pair hanging from pin **4**.

4 Work a French fan with the right worker pair hanging at pin **3**, working through one pair to the right in cloth stitch and twist, and one pair in cloth stitch. Put up pivot pin **6**.

5 When pin **7** has been put up, leave it uncovered.

6 *Work pin **8** in double stitch ground with the left pair from pin **5** and the pair hanging on pivot pin **6**. (To pin up at pin **8**, take the pivot pin **6** out, and re-pin at pin **8**. Gently pull on the left worker pair at pin **7** to flatten the loops at the base of the fan.)

7 Work pin **9** in double stitch ground with the right pair hanging at pin **8** and the pair from pin **5**.

8 Pins **10**, **11** and **12** are worked as for pins **2**, **4** and **5**.

9 Return to the worker pair hanging on the left on pin **7** and work the next fan.**

10 Repeat from * to ** for the required length.

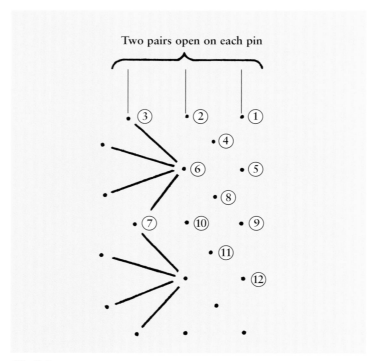

Fig 8.8

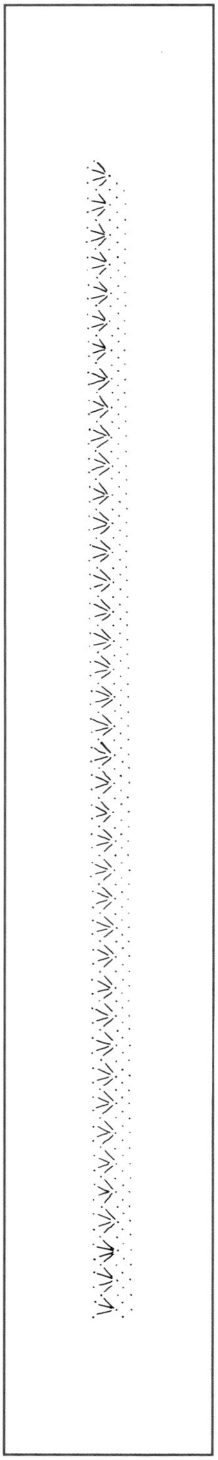

Fig 8.9
Pattern 42

Underwear
INSERTION

FINISHED SIZE 7/32in (5mm) wide

*W*hen this insertion is attached to the underwear, thread through ribbon or stranded embroidery thread and decorate with ribbon bows.

MATERIALS

8 pairs Madeira Tanne 80

Ribbon 1/8in (3.5mm) wide or stranded embroidery thread

ALTERNATIVE THREAD

Brok 100/2

STITCHES USED

Roseground 1   see page 23

Fig 8.10

Method

1 Referring to Fig 8.11, hang four pairs on support pins above the work.

2 Hang two pairs open on pins **1** and **2** and twist each pair.

3 *Work the left pair on pin **1** through three pairs to the right in cloth stitch, twist the workers and put up pin **3**.

4 Take the workers to the left through three pairs in cloth stitch and put up pin **4**.

5 Reversing the instructions, repeat for pins **5** and **6**. *Remove the support pins and pull down the spare thread.*

6 Take the workers at pin **6** through two pairs to the left in cloth stitch, twist the worker pair and the next pair to the left.

7 Repeat on the other side from pin **4**.

8 Now use four pairs to work a roseground as follows:

Work cloth stitch and twist with the two left pairs. *No pin.*

Work cloth stitch and twist with the two right pairs. *No pin.*

With the middle two pairs work half stitch, pin, half stitch at pin **7**.

With the two left pairs work half stitch, pin, half stitch at pin **8**.

With the two right pairs work half stitch, pin, half stitch at pin **9**.

With the middle two pairs work half stitch, pin, half stitch at pin **10**.

Work cloth stitch and twist with the two left pairs. *No pin.*

Work cloth stitch and twist with the two right pairs. *No pin.*

9 Work the third pair from the right to the right through two pairs in cloth stitch. Pin up at **11**.

10 Work the third pair from the left to the left through two pairs in cloth stitch. Pin up at **12**.**

11 Repeat from * to ** for the required length.

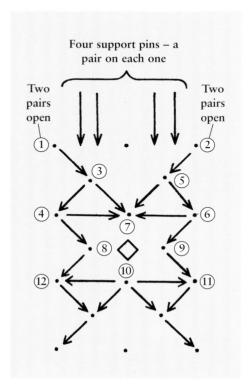

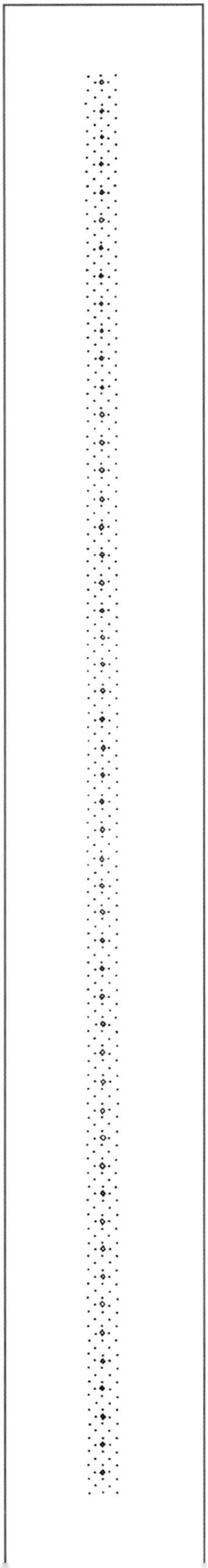

Four support pins – a pair on each one

Two pairs open

Two pairs open

Fig 8.11

Fig 8.12
Pattern 43

Fan 1

FINISHED SIZE ⁹⁄₃₂in (7mm) wide

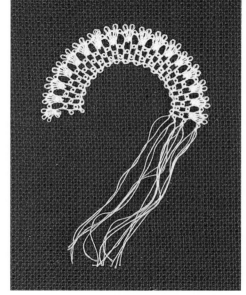

*T*his is the first of two fans for you to try. The
pattern is an adaptation of the underwear edging
on page 109 and is simple to work.

Fig 8.13

MATERIALS

7 pairs DMC Broder Machine 50

PVA glue

Metal fan-shaped jewellery finding

0.4 crochet hook

Fine crochet thread

ALTERNATIVE THREAD

Madeira Tanne 50

STITCHES USED

Double stitch ground	see page 19
French fan	see page 21

METHOD

1 This is worked in the same way as
the underwear edging (see page 109)
with two minor alterations:

- The worker pair in the French fan
  works through two pairs only in
  cloth stitch and twist to the pivot pin
  (see step 4, page 110).

- The ground has more pinholes, and
  there is only one row to work
  between each fan (see steps 6 to 8,
  page 110).

2 When the lace is complete, take it off
the pillow and glue it carefully to the
edge of a metal fan-shaped jewellery
finding, gathering the lace if necessary to
fit the shape.

3 Crochet a tiny cord with fine crochet
thread and attach it to the handle of the
fan, knotting the ends together to form a
small tassel.

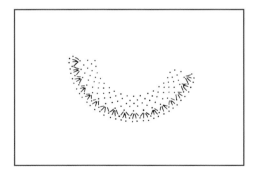

Fig 8.14
Pattern 44

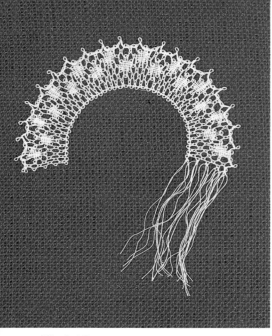

Fig 8.15

Fan 2

FINISHED SIZE ⅜in (1cm) wide

This second fan takes a little more care to work than the first (see page 113), as the thread is finer and the pinholes closer together. It is mounted on a tiny set of fan sticks (see the list of suppliers on page 163).

MATERIALS

11 pairs Egyptian gassed cotton 170/2

Set of fan sticks

PVA glue

0.4 crochet hook

Fine crochet thread

ALTERNATIVE THREAD

Brok 170/2

STITCHES USED

Torchon ground	see page 18
Cloth stitch diamond	see page 19
Plait	see page 148
Picot	see page 148

METHOD

1 Referring to Fig 8.16, hang three pairs side by side on pin **1**.

2 Hang two pairs open on pins **2** to **5**. Twist each pair and cover each pin with a half stitch.

3 Take the left pair at pin **1** through two pairs to the right in cloth stitch, twist the workers and work a Torchon ground stitch at pin **6** with the left pair from pin **2**.

4 Take the left pair at pin **6** through two pairs to the left in cloth stitch and put up pin **7**.

5 Take the workers back through two pairs to the right in cloth stitch, twist them and leave the pair ready to take into the work later.

6 With the two pairs at pin **7**, work a plait to pin **8**, where a picot is worked.

114

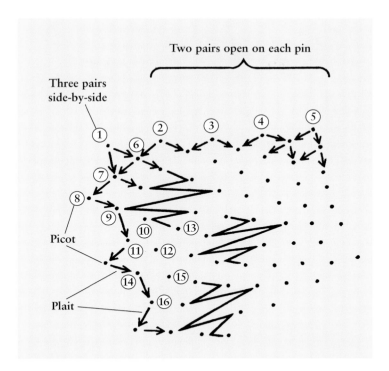

Three pairs side-by-side

Two pairs open on each pin

Picot

Plait

— TIP —

You could extend both these patterns to make pretty little collars (see page 161).

Fig 8.16

7 Work a plait back to pin **9** and leave.

8 Work the cloth stitch diamond. When pin **9** of the diamond is reached, take in the two plait pairs and then leave them out again.

9 When the diamond is complete, the pair from pin **10** is worked to the left through the two pairs hanging from pin **9** in cloth stitch, and pin **11** is put up.

10 Take this pair back to the right through two pairs in cloth stitch, twist, and with the left pair from pin **13** work a Torchon ground stitch in pin **12**.

11 The two pairs from pin **11** work a plait and picot as before.

12 Take the left pair from pin **12** to the left through the two plait pairs in cloth stitch, and pin up at pin **14**.

13 Take the workers back to the right, twist, and work a ground stitch at pin **15**.

14 The left pair at pin **15** now works back to the left through two pairs in cloth stitch; then pin up at pin **16**. Work back to the right and continue the pattern as now set.

15 When the lace is complete, take it off the pillow and glue the lace to the fan sticks.

16 Crochet a cord with tassels, as for the first fan (see step 3, page 113).

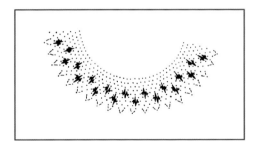

Fig 8.17
Pattern 45

115

Bedside TABLE MAT

FINISHED SIZE 1³⁄₁₆ x 1³⁄₁₆in (3 x 3cm)

N*o home is complete without mats or doilies in every room. Here is another pattern for a mat, this time covering a bedside table.*

Fig 8.18

MATERIALS

14 pairs Madeira Tanne 80

ALTERNATIVE THREAD

Brok 100/2

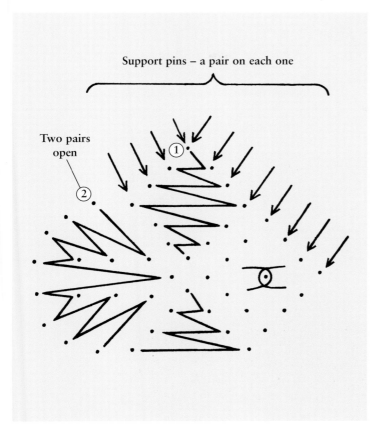

Support pins – a pair on each one

Two pairs open

① ②

Fig 8.19

Torchon ground	see page 18
Cloth stitch diamond	see page 19
Fir tree fan	see page 21
Spider	see page 22

METHOD

1 Hang pairs on support pins above the work and bring them into the work following Fig 8.19.

2 Work the cloth stitch diamond at pin **1** and the spider. *Remove the support pins and pull down the thread.*

3 Hang two pairs open on pin **2** and work the fir tree fan.

4 Complete the work by following the instructions for Working Circular and Square Shapes on page 36.

Fig 8.20 Pattern 46

– TIP –

When moving several bobbins across the pillow at once, use the palm of your hand to prevent the bobbins from jumping out of order.

Large SHAWL

FINISHED SIZE 4¼ x 4¼ x 6in (11 x 11 x 15cm)

Fig 8.21

I like the effect that the blocks of compound spiders give to this large shawl. They create a 'cobweb' appearance which is very effective.

MATERIALS

57 pairs Madeira Tanne 80

ALTERNATIVE THREAD
Brok 100/2

STITCHES USED

Torchon ground	see page 18
Cloth stitch diamond	see page 19
Fir tree fan	see page 21
Spider	see page 22
Cloth stitch trail	see page 25
Compound spiders	see page 156

METHOD

1 Begin working the lace by following Fig 8.22. Pairs are added at each circled pin.

2 Fig 8.23 shows how to finish the shawl. Pairs are taken into the cloth stitch trail from each circled pin.

Refer to the instructions for the table mat edgings on page 70, as the method of starting and finishing the shawl is similar.

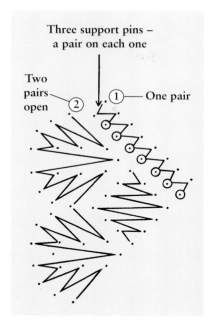

Fig 8.22

Fig 8.23

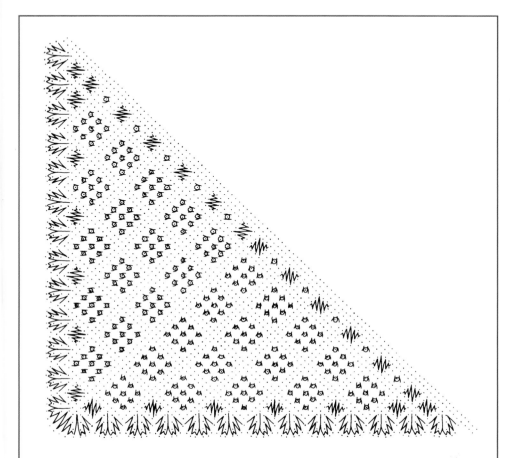

— *TIP* —

The large safety-pin stitch-holders used in knitting are useful for keeping your bobbins in order when not in use. Thread the pin end through the spangle loops, close the pin and your bobbins will be kept safely in order until they are needed.

Fig 8.24
Pattern 47

Circular
TABLECLOTH

FINISHED SIZE 5⅛in (13cm) diameter

*T*his design would
complement any room setting,
but it looks particularly
appropriate in the bedroom
with a breakfast tray ready for
the lady of the house. The
edging is also used on the table
in the lacemaker's cottage (see
page ii).

MATERIALS

28 pairs Madeira Tanne 80

ALTERNATIVE THREAD

Brok 100/2

Fig 8.25

STITCHES USED

Torchon ground	see page 18
Torchon footside	see page 18
Fir tree fan	see page 21
Roseground 1	see page 23
Cloth stitch trail	see page 25

METHOD

1 Make extra pinholes across the two trails to start the pattern: see pins **A** and **B** in Fig 8.26.

2 Hang pairs on support pins above the work and bring them into the work as it progresses.

3 Start with the cloth stitch trail at pin **1**, bringing in new pairs from support pins until pin **2** is reached.

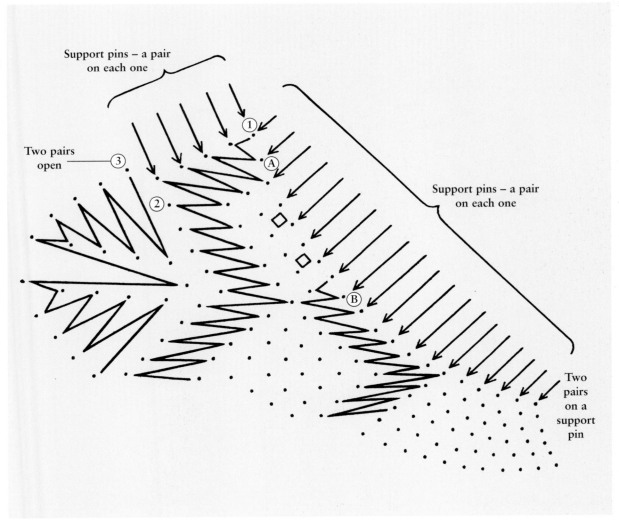

Fig 8.26

4 Start the fir tree fan at pin **3**. Make sure that the workers to the left at pin **3** are wound with plenty of thread.

5 Roseground is worked in the first area inside the cloth stitch trail. This alternates with Torchon ground around the edging.

– TIP –

When working the ground, you may find it easier to work each row from the inside to the footside edge.

6 Start the second trail, bringing in pairs from the support pins on the right.

7 Continue the pattern as now set.

8 To make the tablecloth hang realistically, follow the tip given for the jug cover on page 57.

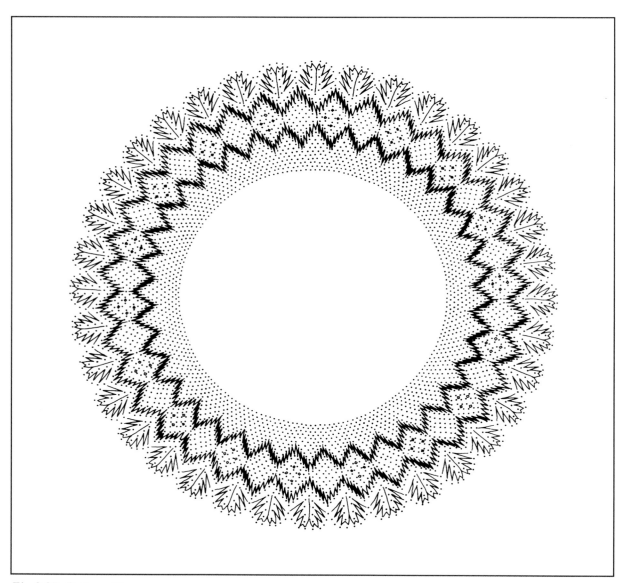

Fig 8.27 Pattern 48

Bedspread

FINISHED SIZE One strip measures ¾ x 6in (2 x 15cm)

*B*ecause the bedspread is worked in strips, it is
easily adapted for a single or double bed. Narrow
and wide edgings are provided, so that you can
choose which combination best fits your bed.

Fig 8.28

MATERIALS

NARROW EDGING

25 pairs Madeira Tanne 80

WIDE EDGING

45 pairs Madeira Tanne 80

STRIP 1

25 pairs Madeira Tanne 80

STRIPS 2 TO 5

23 pairs Madeira Tanne 80

STRIP 6

24 pairs Madeira Tanne 80

ALTERNATIVE THREAD

Brok 100/2

STITCHES USED

Torchon ground	see page 18
Torchon footside	see page 18
Pinhole ground	see page 19
Fir tree fan	see page 21
Cloth stitch trail	see page 25
Square tally	see page 152
Eyed spider	see page 156

METHOD

The tallies in the ground can be omitted. Make a ground stitch where they would have been worked.

EDGINGS (Fig 8.29)

1 Refer to Fig 8.29 to start the edging. At pin **1** the two workers work together.

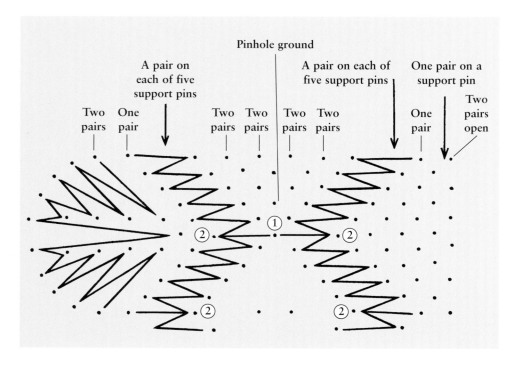

Fig 8.29

2 At pin **2** the pinhole is used twice (back stitch). Take the pin out and re-pin it under the worker pair in the same hole. (Be careful not to pull on the workers too much, or they will pull the passive pairs away from pin **2** and create a hole in the cloth stitch trail.)

STARTING STRIP 1
(Footside left and top: Fig 8.29)

1 This strip is started in the same way as the curtains on page 82, but pin **1** will have five pairs open to start. Cloth stitch and twist the left two pairs and twist the other three pairs once.

2 Put up pin **2** under the right pair. Hang two pairs open on it, and continue along the top pinholes as for the curtains on page 82. The last pinhole has no pairs hanging on it. Put up the last pin under the right pair.

3 Work the second pair from the left to the right through all the pairs in cloth stitch and twist. Knot the last pair worked through twice up to the pin.

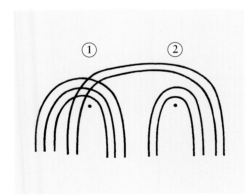

Fig 8.30

FINISHING STRIP 1 (Fig 8.31)

1 Try to keep good tension. Work down the strip until the bottom row of holes remains.

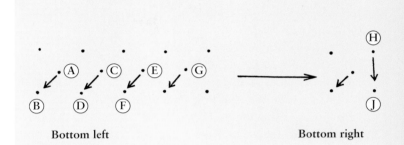

Bottom left   Bottom right

Fig 8.31

2 Knot each pair twice. Two pairs hang from each pin and one pair hangs on the bottom right pin **H**.

3 Work the left pair from **A** to the left through one pair in cloth stitch, twist once and work cloth stitch and twist with the outside pair.

4 Pin up under two pairs in **B** and cover with a cloth stitch.

5 Work the left pair from **C** to the left through three pairs in cloth stitch, twist once and work a cloth stitch and twist with the outside pair. Put up pin **D** under two pairs and cover with a cloth stitch.

6 *Work the left pair from **E** to the left through five pairs in cloth stitch, twist once and work a cloth stitch and twist with the outside pair. Put up pin **F** under two pairs and cover with cloth stitch.

7 Knot and throw back the next two pairs to the right.

8 Take the left pair from **G** and continue from * along the bottom row.

9 At the last pinhole on the right, take the pair hanging from **H** and work to the left through five pairs as usual.

10 Pin up at **J**, cover, knot and throw back two pairs (five pairs left).

11 Knot each pair. These pairs will be needed for the bottom of strip 2, so leave them with long threads. Cut all the other thrown-out threads close to the work. Keep at least three rows of pins in on the right-hand side of strip 1 plus all the other footside pins. Push these pins down flush to the pillow and cover with a cloth to prevent the pins from snagging on the working threads.

STARTING STRIP 2
(Footside along top)

1 Sew in three pairs into the top right hole of strip 1. (Take a pair of bobbins and pull a loop through the hole with a crochet hook. Pass one of the bobbins through this loop and pull up. Repeat for the other two pairs. Replace the pin.) Cloth stitch and twist the two right pairs.

2 Put a pin in the top left hole of strip 2, under the right pair from strip 1.

3 Hang two pairs open on this pin.

4 Twist the left pair once, and cloth stitch and twist the right two pairs.

5 *Put a pin in the next pinhole to the right, under the right pair, and hang two pairs open on this pin.

6 Twist the left pair once, and cloth stitch and twist the right two pairs.

7 Repeat from * in all the pinholes along the top. (The last hole has no pairs hanging, just put up the last pin under the right pair.)

8 With the remaining sewn-in pair from the top right pinhole of strip 1, work through all the pairs to the right in cloth stitch and twist.

9 Knot the last pair worked through twice up to the pin.

10 As you work strip 2, make sewings into strip 1 on the left side.

FINISHING STRIP 2 (Fig 8.32)
1 Work down the strip until the bottom row of holes remains.

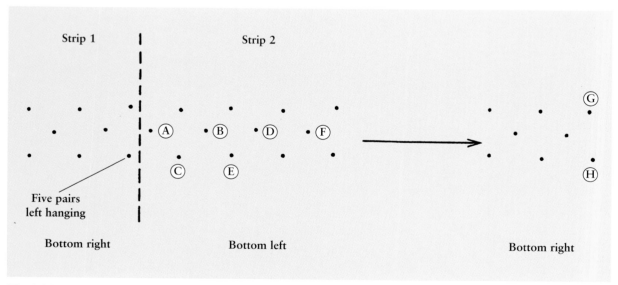

Fig 8.32

2 Knot each pair twice. Two pairs hang from each pin and one pair hangs on bottom right pin **G**.

3 The five pairs left at the bottom of strip 1 must now be taken back into the work. Twist the left pair once.

4 Take the left pair from pin **A** to the left through four of the pairs from strip 1 in cloth stitch.

5 Sew this pair into the bottom right pinhole of strip 1 and knot. Lay it back down to the right of the twisted pair.

6 Work the left pair from **B** to the left through six pairs in cloth stitch. Twist once and work a cloth stitch and twist with the outside pair. Put up pin **C** under two pairs and cover with cloth stitch.

7 Knot and throw out the next three pairs to the right.

8 *Work the left pair from **D** to the left through five pairs in cloth stitch. Twist once and work cloth stitch and twist with the outside pair. Put up pin **E** under two pairs and cover with cloth stitch.

9 Knot and throw out the next two pairs to the right.

10 Take the left pair from **F** and continue from * along the bottom row.

11 At the last pinhole on the right, take the pair hanging from **G** and work to the left through five pairs as usual.

12 Pin up at **H**, cover, knot and throw back two pairs (five pairs left).

13 Knot each pair. These pairs will be needed for the bottom of strip 3, so leave them with long threads. Cut all the other thrown-out threads close to the work.

STRIPS 3, 4 AND 5
(Footside along top)

1 Start and finish these strips in the same way as for strip 2.

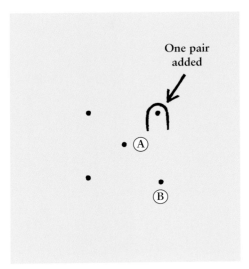

Fig 8.33

STRIP 6 (Footside along top and right side; Fig 8.33)

1 Start this strip as for strips 2 to 5. At the top right pin, hang one pair only under the right pair and cloth stitch and twist them together.

2 With the remaining sewn-in pair from the right pinhole of strip 5, work through all the pairs to the right in cloth stitch and twist.

3 At the top right side of strip 6, work half stitch, pin, half stitch at pin **A**, and a footside pin at **B**, pinning up under two pairs.

FINISHING STRIP 6

1 Finish at the bottom as for strips 2 to 5, up to the last pin on the bottom right. There will be eight pairs.

2 Take the third pair from the left through four pairs to the right in cloth stitch, twist once, and work a cloth stitch and twist with the outside pair.

3 Pin up under two pairs in the last pinhole.

4 Work the small tab in cloth stitch, throwing out one pair on each row until there are five pairs left.

5 Knot each pair twice and cut the threads.

6 Take the lace off the pillow, fold the tab back onto the wrong side and sew in place.

7 Sew the two edgings on either side.

> **— TIP —**
>
> *The bedspread can also be worked in separate strips, and then sewn together with a needle and thread.*

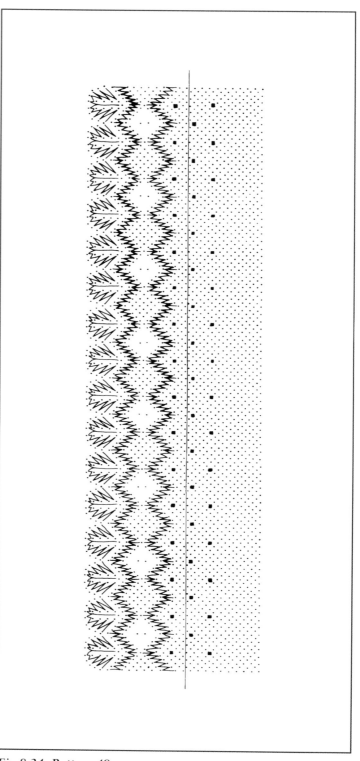

Fig 8.34 Pattern 49

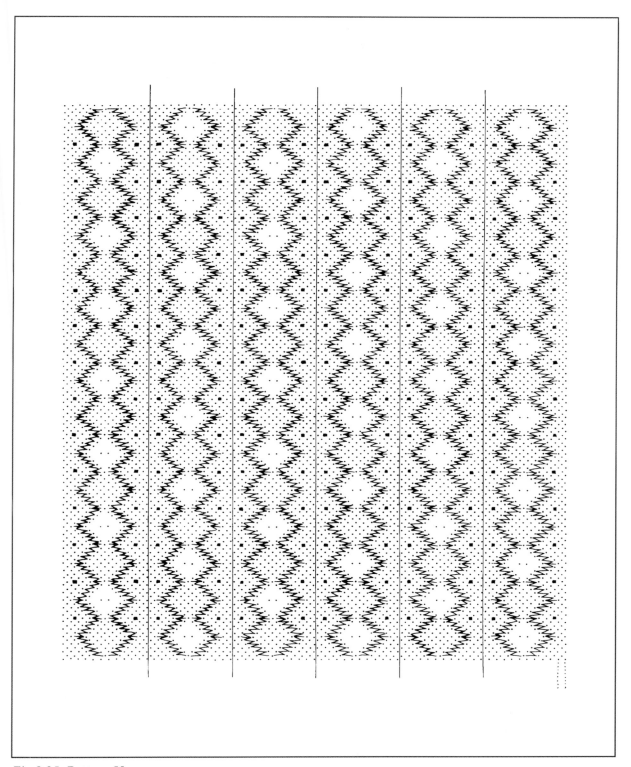

Fig 8.35 Pattern 50

The
NURSERY

The hand-painted nursery furniture is original and is the copyright of Lyndel Smith.

Fig 9.1

Bath towel
EDGING

FINISHED SIZE ¼ and ⅜in (6 and 9mm) wide

I have worked two sizes of this pattern. The lacemaker on page ii is working the mini version. Here in the nursery the larger edging is used to decorate the bath towels.

MATERIALS

LARGE EDGING

9 pairs DMC Broder Machine 50

Fine towelling material

ALTERNATIVE THREAD

Madeira Tanne 50

MINI EDGING

8 pairs Egyptian gassed cotton 170/2

Duchesse pins

ALTERNATIVE THREAD

Brok 170/2

STITCHES USED

Torchon footside	see page 18
Torchon ground	see page 18
Cloth stitch fan	see page 20

METHOD

1 Referring to Fig 9.3, hang two pairs open on pins **1**, **2**, **3** and **4**. Hang one pair on a support pin above the work.

2 Twist each pair on pin **2** and cover with a half stitch.

3 Repeat with the pairs on pin **3**.

4 Twist each pair on pin **4** and cover with a cloth stitch and twist.

5 Work the left pair on pin **4** to the left through one pair on a support pin in cloth stitch and twist.

Fig 9.2

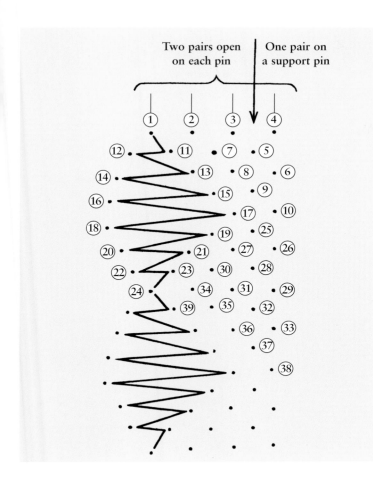

Fig 9.3

10 Work pin **8** in Torchon ground stitch with the right pair from pin **7** and the left pair from pin **5**.

11 Work pin **9** in Torchon ground stitch with the right pair from pin **8** and the left pair from pin **6**.

12 Take the right pair hanging at pin **9** through two pairs to the right in cloth stitch and twist. Pin up under two at pin **10** and cover the pin with cloth stitch and twist.

13 Twist each pair on pin **1** and cover the pin with cloth stitch.

14 *The right pair hanging on pin **1** is the worker pair for the fan. Take the workers through the next pair from pin **2** in cloth stitch, twist the workers and pin up at **11**.

15 Work in cloth stitch through two pairs to the left, twist the workers, and put up pin **12**.

16 Work in cloth stitch through three pairs to the right, twist the workers, and put up pin **13**.

17 Work in cloth stitch through three pairs to the left, twist the workers, and put up pin **14**.

18 Work in cloth stitch through four pairs to the right, twist the workers, and put up pin **15**.

19 Work in cloth stitch through four pairs to the left, twist the workers, and put up pin **16**.

20 Work in cloth stitch through five pairs to the right, twist the workers, and put up pin **17**.

21 Work in cloth stitch through five pairs to the left, twist the workers, and put up pin **18**.

6 Work through the next pair to the left in half stitch and put up pin **5**. Cover with half stitch.

7 Take the right pair hanging at pin **5** through two pairs to the right in cloth stitch and twist. Pin up under two pairs at pin **6** (pin up under two means to the left of the two pairs just worked) (Torchon footside). Cover pin **6** with a cloth stitch and twist. *Remove the support pins and pull down the spare thread.*

8 Work pin **7** in half stitch, pin, half stitch (Torchon ground) with the right pair from pin **2** and the left pair from pin **3**.

9 Take out the support pin and pull the loop of thread down to the work.

– TIP –

When tensioning the work, hold the passive pairs with one hand while pulling gently on the worker pair with the other hand.

22 Work in cloth stitch through four pairs to the right, twist the workers, and put up pin **19**.

23 Work in cloth stitch through four pairs to the left, twist the workers, and put up pin **20**.

24 Work in cloth stitch through three pairs to the right, twist the workers, and put up pin **21**.

25 Work in cloth stitch through three pairs to the left, twist the workers, and put up pin **22**.

26 Work in cloth stitch through two pairs to the right, twist the workers, and put up pin **23**.

27 Work in cloth stitch through two pairs to the left, twist the workers, and put up pin **24**. Cover pin **24** with cloth stitch.

28 Work Torchon ground stitch at pin **25**.

29 Work Torchon footside at pin **26**.

30 Work Torchon ground stitch at pins **27** and **28**.

31 Work Torchon footside at pin **29**.

32 Work Torchon ground stitch at pins **30**, **31** and **32**.

33 Work Torchon footside at pin **33**.

34 Work Torchon ground stitch at pins **34**, **35**, **36** and **37**.

35 Work Torchon footside at pin **38**.**

36 Repeat from * to ** for the required length.

The fans can all be worked in cloth stitch as described above, but they can also be worked in half stitch as shown in the photograph on page 132, where cloth stitch and half stitch fans have been worked alternately. The half stitch fans are worked with the outside edge pair worked in cloth stitch and twist before and after the pin. The mini edging is worked with a Torchon ground stitch instead of a Torchon footside edge.

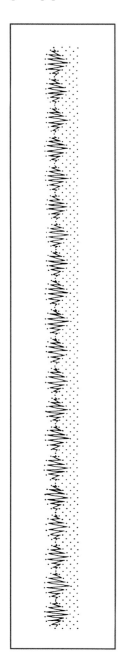

Fig 9.4 RIGHT
Pattern 51

Fig 9.5 FAR RIGHT
Pattern 52

Nursery MAT

FINISHED SIZE 1in (2.5cm) square

*A*nother example of this easy-to-work mat appears in the lacemaker's cottage on page ii.

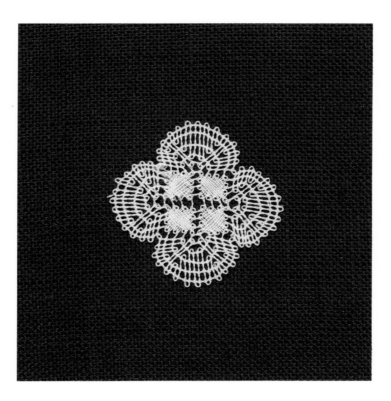

Fig 9.6

MATERIALS

10 pairs Madeira Tanne 80

ALTERNATIVE THREAD

Brok 100/2

135

STITCHES USED

Cloth stitch diamond	see page 19
Fir tree fan	see page 21

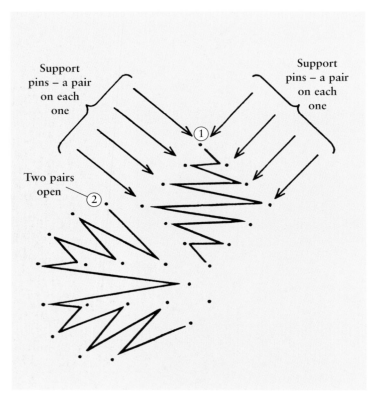

Support pins – a pair on each one

Support pins – a pair on each one

Two pairs open

Fig 9.7

METHOD

1 Referring to Fig 9.7, hang eight pairs on support pins above the work. Hang two pairs open on pin **2**.

2 Start the cloth stitch diamond at pin **1**, bringing in pairs from the support pins on left and right. *Remember to remove the support pins and pull down the spare thread as the work progresses.*

3 Start the fir tree fan at pin **2**.

4 Complete the work by following the instructions for Working Circular and Square Shapes on page 36.

Fig 9.8 Pattern 53

Baby dress
TRIM

FINISHED SIZE $^7/_{32}$in (5mm) wide

*T*he bridge fan used on this trimming creates a pretty frilly edging, which is just right for a baby's dress.

MATERIALS

5 pairs Madeira Tanne 80

ALTERNATIVE THREAD

Brok 100/2

STITCHES USED

Torchon ground	see page 18
Bridge fan	(see instructions on page 138)

Fig 9.9

METHOD

1 Referring to Fig 9.10, hang two pairs open on pins **1** and **2**. Twist each pair and cover each pin with a half stitch.

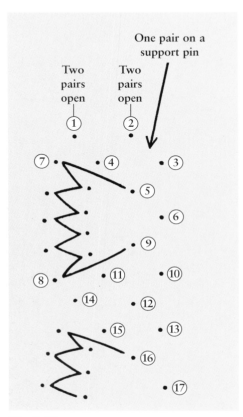

One pair on a support pin

Two pairs open

Two pairs open

Fig 9.10

2 Hang one pair on a support pin above the work, to the right of pin **2**. Work a half stitch with the right pair hanging on pin **2** and the pair on the support pin. Pin up at **3** and cover the pin with a half stitch.

3 Work a Torchon ground stitch at pin **4** with the right pair from pin **1** and the left pair from pin **2**.

4 Work pins **5** and **6** as for pin **4**. *Remove the support pin and pull down the spare thread.*

5 *Take the pair from pin **5** as the worker pair and work to the left through two pairs in cloth stitch and twist. Pin up at pin **7**.

6 Work the fan through two passive pairs in cloth stitch and twist to pin **8** and put up the pin.

7 Take the workers to the right through two pairs in cloth stitch and twist. Work through the next pair to the right in half stitch and put up pin **9**. Cover the pin with a half stitch.

8 Work pins **10** to **17** in Torchon ground stitch.**

9 Work from * to ** for the required length.

Fig 9.11
Pattern 54

Small SHAWL

FINISHED SIZE   2½ x 2½ x 3⅜in (6.5 x 6.5 x 8.5cm)

*T*he grandma here and the lacemaker on page ii are wearing this shawl. Secure the shawl around your doll's neck with a pretty bead as a brooch.

MATERIALS

37 pairs Madeira Tanne 80

ALTERNATIVE THREAD

Brok 100/2

Fig 9.12

STITCHES USED

Torchon ground	see page 18
Cloth stitch diamond	see page 19
Cloth stitch fan with cloth stitch and twist edge	see page 20
Spider	see page 22

METHOD

1 Start working the lace by referring to Fig 9.13. Pairs are added at each circled pin.

2 Refer to the instructions for the table mat edgings on page 70 and the large shawl on page 118 as the method of starting and finishing the small shawl is similar.

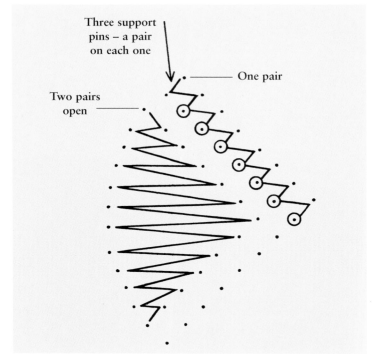

Three support pins – a pair on each one

One pair

Two pairs open

Fig 9.13

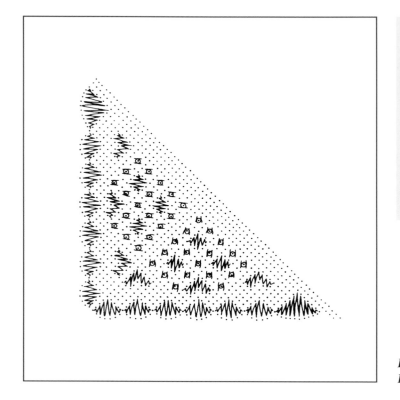

Fig 9.14
Pattern 55

– TIP –

Give yourself plenty of working room by pushing the bobbins not in use to either side of the pillow and securing them in place with divider pins.

Girl's PARTY DRESS

FINISHED SIZE See list of materials for measurements

*T*he underskirt frill of this little girl's party dress uses a wide edging made with a half stitch trail, while the top skirt frill uses a medium edging made with a cloth stitch trail. A simple edging is used for the sleeve ruffle and as the skirt for her doll. Around the neck of both the little girl and her doll is a gathered length of the bedlinen edging featured on page 106, which is also used to decorate the underwear.

Fig 9.15

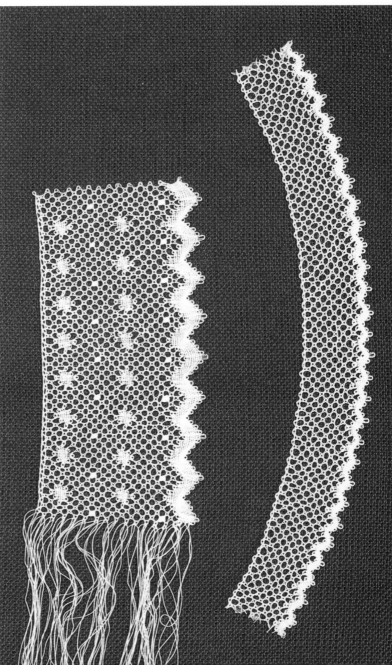

COLLAR (1IN/2.5CM SQUARE)

12 pairs Egyptian gassed cotton 120/2

SIMPLE EDGING (⅝IN/1.5CM WIDE)

16 pairs Egyptian gassed cotton 120/2

MEDIUM EDGING (1¼IN/3.2CM WIDE)

32 pairs Egyptian gassed cotton 120/2
(Half stitch)

34 pairs Egyptian gassed cotton 120/2
(Cloth stitch)

WIDE EDGING (2½IN/6.5CM WIDE)

64 pairs Egyptian gassed cotton 120/2
(Half stitch)

66 pairs Egyptian gassed cotton 120/2
(Cloth stitch)

ALTERNATIVE THREAD

Brok 120/2

STITCHES USED

Torchon ground	see page 18
Torchon footside	see page 18
Cloth stitch diamond	see page 19
Cloth stitch or half stitch trail	see page 25
Square tally	see page 152

METHOD

When working the trail in cloth stitch, there will be eight passive pairs and one worker pair. When working the trail in half stitch, there will be six passive pairs and one worker pair.

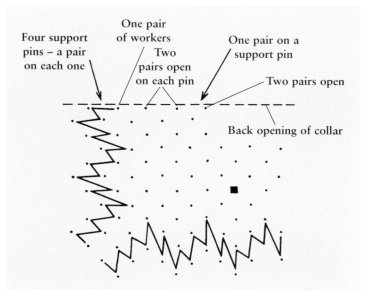

Fig 9.16

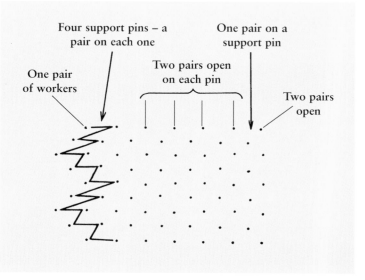

Fig 9.17

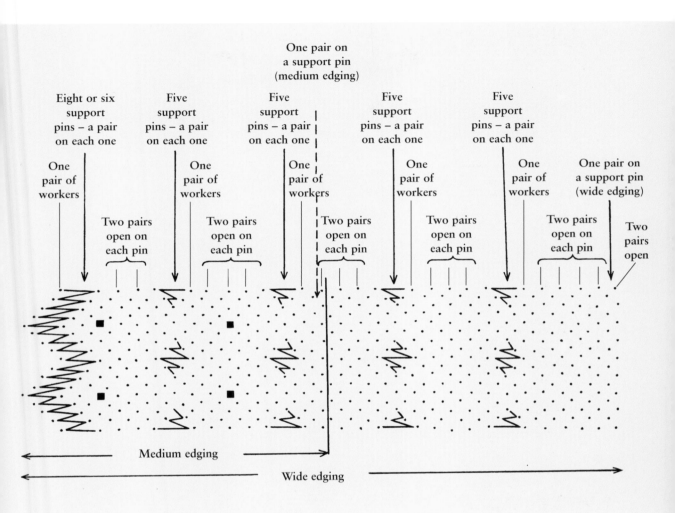

One pair on
a support pin
(medium edging)

Eight or six
support
pins – a pair
on each one

Five
support
pins – a pair
on each one

Five
support
pins – a pair
on each one

Five
support
pins – a pair
on each one

Five
support
pins – a pair
on each one

One pair on
a support pin
(wide edging)

One
pair of
workers

One
pair of
workers

One
pair of
workers

One
pair of
workers

One
pair of
workers

Two pairs
open on
each pin

Two pairs
open on
each pin

Two pairs
open on
each pin

Two pairs
open on
each pin

Two pairs
open on
each pin

Two
pairs
open

Medium edging

Wide edging

Fig 9.18

COLLAR (Fig 9.19: Pattern 56)
Start the work at the back opening of
the collar, referring to Fig 9.16.

SIMPLE EDGING (Fig 9.20:
Pattern 57)
Start the work referring to Fig 9.17.

MEDIUM AND WIDE EDGINGS
(Fig 9.21: Pattern 58)
Start the work referring to Fig 9.18.

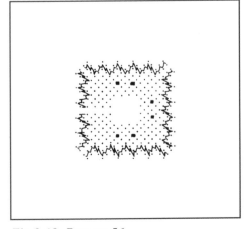

Fig 9.19 Pattern 56

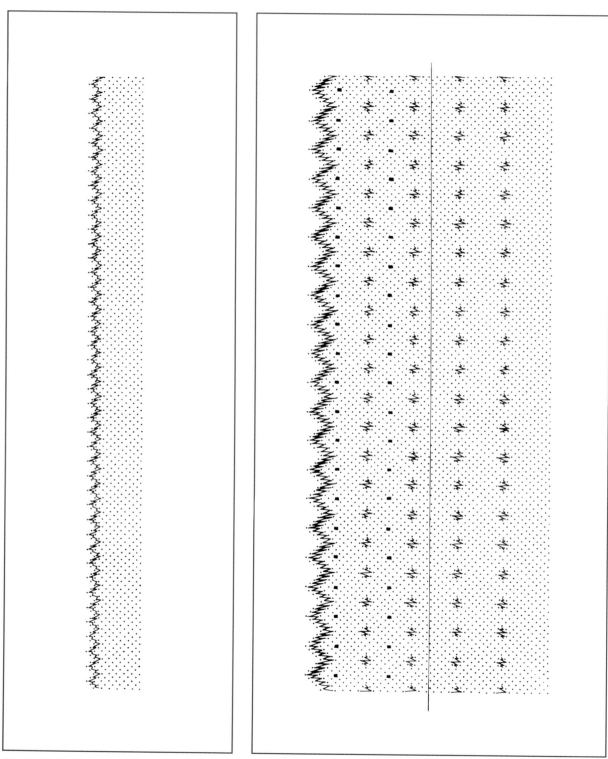

Fig 9.20 Pattern 57

Fig 9.21 Pattern 58

Crib HANGINGS

FINISHED SIZE   1¾ and 2¼in (4.5 and 5.7cm)

*E*very mother would enjoy 'showing off' her
newborn baby sleeping in a lovely crib, trimmed
with delicate lace hangings. I am sure that your
dolls' house mother would be no exception.

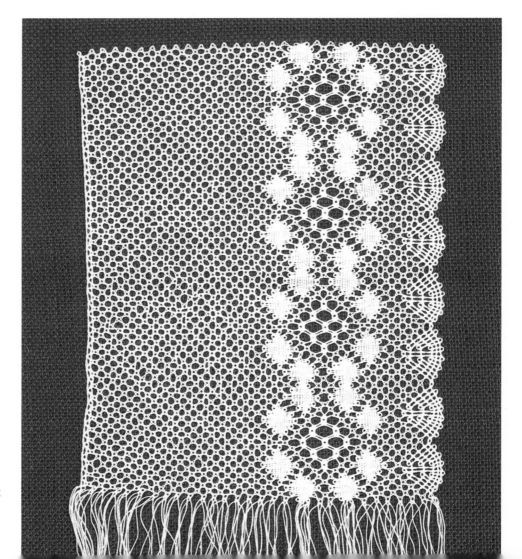

Fig 9.22

MATERIALS

NARROW EDGING

45 pairs Madeira Tanne 80

WIDE EDGING

63 pairs Madeira Tanne 80

Milliner's elastic (thin)

Silk ribbon

ALTERNATIVE THREAD

Brok 100/2

STITCHES USED

Torchon ground	see page 18
Torchon footside	see page 18
Cloth stitch diamond	see page 19
Fir tree fan	see page 21
Compound spider	see page 156

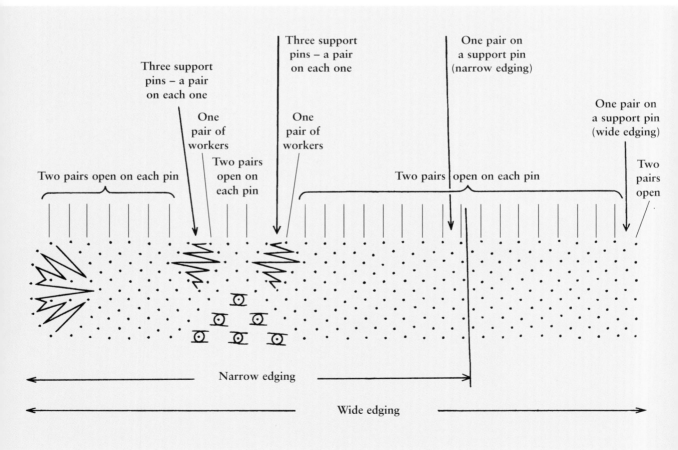

Three support pins – a pair on each one

One pair of workers

Two pairs open on each pin

Three support pins – a pair on each one

One pair of workers

One pair on a support pin (narrow edging)

One pair on a support pin (wide edging)

Two pairs open on each pin

Two pairs open on each pin

Two pairs open

Narrow edging

Wide edging

Fig 9.23

METHOD

Calculate the length of narrow edging needed for your crib by measuring around the top of the bassinet: you will need one and a half times this measurement. Calculate the length of wide edging needed for the canopy by taking a measurement from floor to floor on either side of the crib over the canopy support bar.

1 Start the pattern by referring to Fig 9.23.

2 The fir tree fan is squatter in shape than usual, so there is an extra passive pair between the two outside pins.

3 Thread thin milliner's elastic through the footside of the narrow edging and attach the lace with ribbon bows around the top edge of the crib.

4 Fold the wide edging in half widthways and sew the footside edges together. Run a gathering thread across the width of the lace at the top and pull it up to fit the canopy support bar. Hang the canopy over the bar and decorate with ribbon bows.

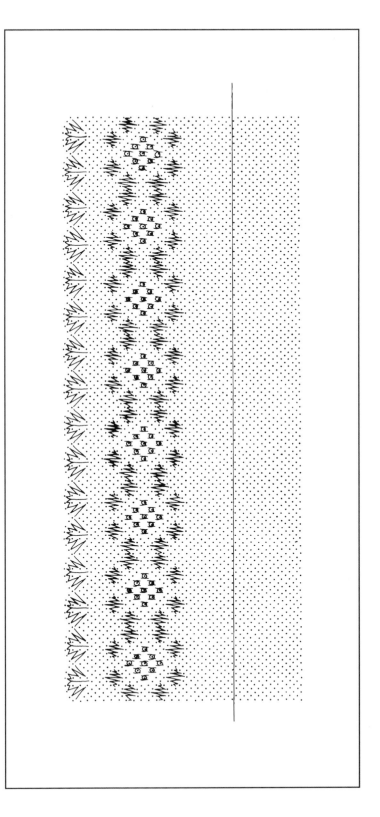

Fig 9.24
Pattern 59

CHAPTER TEN

FURTHER STITCHES
and TECHNIQUES

This final chapter explains some additional stitches and techniques you will need in order to work the more complex patterns in the book.

ADDITIONAL STITCHES

PLAIT (Fig 10.1)

A plait is made with two pairs of bobbins that are worked as a continuous half stitch. Tension well between each stitch.

PICOTS

Picots are usually worked on plaits. Single picots, usually worked with thick threads, work well at miniature scales.

PICOTS ON LEFT

Hold the left pair of the plait taut in your left hand. Take a pin in your right hand. Place the pin horizontally under the right thread and over the left thread (see Fig 10.2). Turn the pin so that the left thread is pulled under the right thread, crossing them (see Fig 10.3). Bring the point of the pin towards you over the crossed threads (see Fig 10.4). Turn the point away under the crossed threads and up between them (see Fig 10.5). Put the pin in the pinhole on the left of the plait and pull the pair up carefully so that the single thread forms a loop around the pin (see Fig 10.6). Twist the left picot pair twice and continue with the plait.

PICOTS ON RIGHT

Work as above, using the right plait pair and reversing the instructions.

If you are working a picot on both sides of the plait, work the first picot, work a half stitch with the two plait pairs, and then work the second picot on the other side. Continue with the plait.

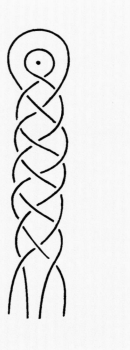

Fig 10.1 Plait.

Fig 10.2

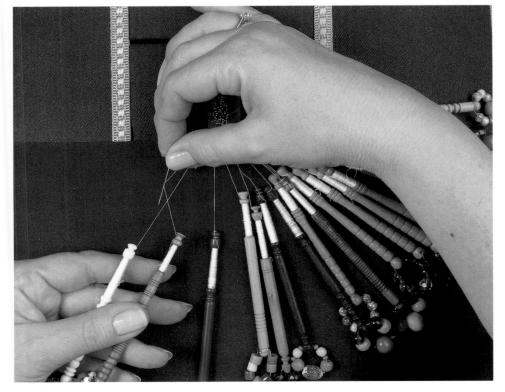

Fig 10.3

Fig 10.4

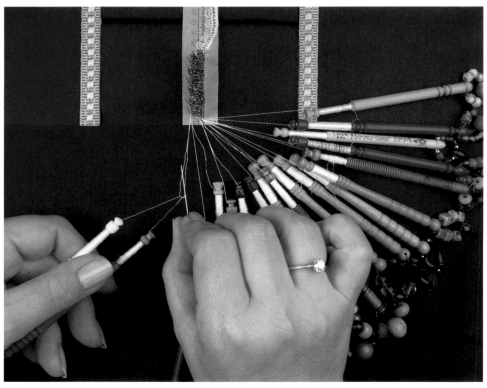

Fig 10.5

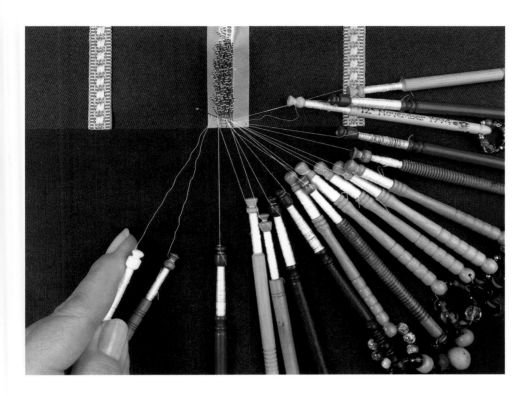

Fig 10.6

LEAF (Fig 10.7)

A leaf is worked with two pairs. Try to use bobbins that are evenly matched in size and weight. Give yourself plenty of space while working by pushing the other bobbins to each side of the pillow. Aim for a tight start and finish.

Cloth stitch the two pairs together and put up a pin in the middle. Take the second bobbin from the left as the weaver, and lengthen it so that the thread will be loose while working. Take the weaver bobbin to the left first, over and under the left thread. Then take it over and under the two pairs to the right. Take the weaver bobbin back to the left over, under and over the three threads to the left. Take the weaver bobbin over and under the two pairs to the right. The weaver bobbin is now back on the right. Tension the shape by pulling the weaver bobbin up and

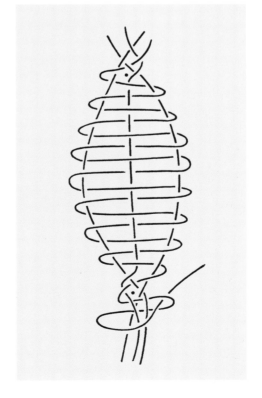

Fig 10.7 Leaf.

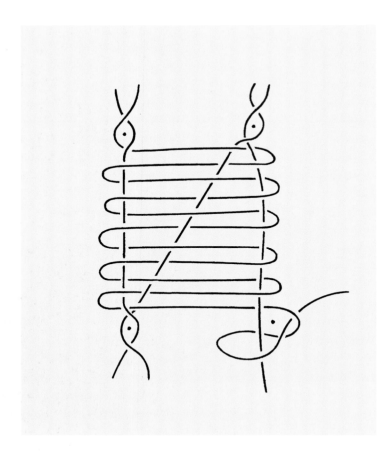

Fig 10.8 Square tally.

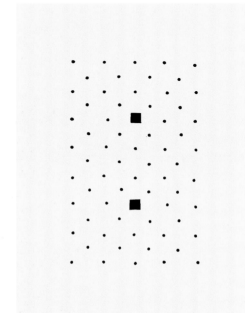

Fig 10.9 Square tally as shown on the pricking.

outwards to the pin, while holding the other bobbins in your left hand.

The outside bobbins control the shape of the leaf. Tension the shape each time the weaver is at the right. Do not pull the weaver at any other time, and remember to hold the edge bobbins taut or the shape will distort. To secure the shape, pin up in the middle of the two pairs and work a hitch with the weaver bobbin over the other three threads (this is my own little trick; it is not strictly 'correct'.) Be careful how you use the weaver bobbin for the next few stitches.

Do not be discouraged if your first attempt fails to achieve a smooth shape. This technique takes a little patience and plenty of practice to perfect.

SQUARE TALLY
(Figs 10.8 and 10.9)

The technique for working a tally is similar to that for working a leaf (see page 151). It is started from two pins because a square shape is required.

Start with the second bobbin from the left as the weaver, lengthen it, and weave as for the leaf shape, this time keeping the outside bobbins straight when tensioning the weaver. When the shape is complete and the weaver bobbin is on the right, work a hitch with it over the right thread to secure the shape. Be very careful how you use the weaver bobbin for the next few stitches. Take any tension off, to minimize the risk of pulling the tally out of shape.

As with the leaf, this technique requires plenty of practice to perfect.

RAISED LEAF
(Figs 10.10 and 10.11)

Work the diamond in cloth or half stitch to pin **1**. Put up pin **2** in the middle of

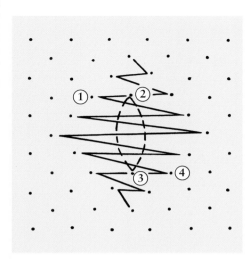

Fig 10.10 Raised leaf.

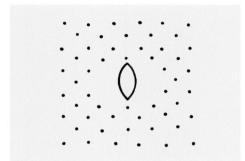

Fig 10.11 Raised leaf as shown on the pricking.

two pairs adjacent to the pin, and work a leaf (see page 151) to pin 3. Take the worker pair left at pin 1 and continue to work with it over the leaf just worked. After pin 4, incorporate the leaf pairs back into the work and complete the shape.

FOUR PAIR CROSSING
(Fig 10.12)

This crossing is worked with four pairs of bobbins, using two threads as one. Work the crossing as follows:

Half stitch, pin, cross middle pairs left over right.

SIX PAIR CROSSING (Fig 10.13)

This crossing is worked with six pairs of bobbins, using two threads as one.

1 Take the centre left pair under the next pair to the left.

2 Take the centre right pair over the next pair to the right.

3 Twist the centre pairs right over left.

4 Take the centre left pair to the left under and over the next two pairs.

5 Take the centre right pair to the right over and under the next two pairs.

6 Put up the pin in centre.

7 Repeat steps 1, 2 and 3.

8 Take the centre left pair under the next pair to the left.

9 Take the centre right pair over the next pair to the right.

10 Ease up carefully.

EIGHT PAIR CROSSING
(Fig 10.14)

This crossing is worked with eight pairs of bobbins, using two threads as one.

1 Work half stitch with the centre four pairs.

Fig 10.12 Four pair crossing.

Fig 10.13 Six pair crossing.

Fig 10.14 Eight pair crossing.

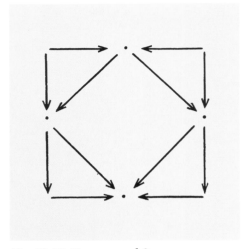

Fig 10.15 Roseground 2.

2 Work half stitch with the right four pairs.

3 Work half stitch with the left four pairs.

4 Repeat steps 1, 2 and 3.

5 Put up the centre pin.

6 Work cloth stitch with the centre four pairs.

7 With the left four pairs, cross centre left over centre right.

8 With the right four pairs, cross centre left over centre right.

9 Ease up carefully.

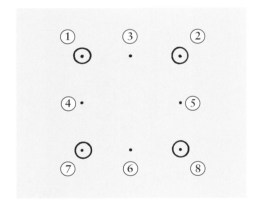

Fig 10.16 Working roseground 2.

ROSEGROUND 2
(Figs 10.15 and 10.16)

Work this stitch in number order (four pairs used):

- Numbers **1** and **2** – half stitch. *No pin*.
- Pinholes **3**, **4**, **5** and **6** – half stitch, pin, half stitch.
- Numbers **7** and **8** – half stitch. *No pin*.

ROSEGROUND 3 (Fig 10.17)

Work in diagonal rows in this sequence (four pairs used):

- Numbers **1** and **2** – half stitch. *No pin*.
- Pinholes **3** and **5** – half stitch, pin, half stitch.

Work half stitch with the two middle pairs between pins **4** and **5**.

- Pinholes **4** and **6** – half stitch, pin, half stitch.
- Numbers **7** and **8** – half stitch. *No pin*.

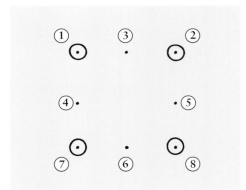

Fig 10.17 Working roseground 3.

ROSEGROUND 4 (Fig 10.18)

Work in number order (four pairs used):

- Numbers **1** and **2** – half stitch. *No pin.*
- Pinhole **3** – half stitch, pin, half stitch.
- Pinholes **4** and **5** – half stitch. *No pin.*
- Pinhole **6** – half stitch, pin, half stitch.
- Numbers **7** and **8** – half stitch. *No pin.*

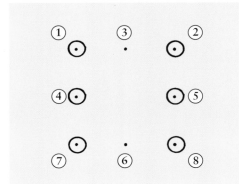

Fig 10.18 Working roseground 4.

ROSEGROUND 5 (Fig 10.19)

Work in number order (four pairs used):

- Numbers **1** and **2** – half stitch and twist. *No pin.*

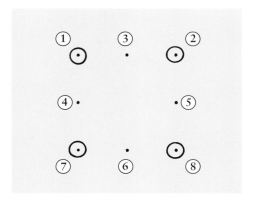

Fig 10.19 Working roseground 5.

- Pinhole **3** – half stitch and twist, pin, half stitch and twist.
- Pinholes **4** and **5** – half stitch, twist outside pair, pin.

Work half stitch with the two middle pairs between pins **4** and **5**.

- Pinholes **4** and **5** – cover pins with half stitch, twist outside pairs.
- Pinhole **6** – half stitch and twist, pin, half stitch and twist.
- Numbers **7** and **8** – half stitch and twist. *No pin.*

BIAS GROUND 1 (Fig 10.20)

Work in diagonal rows. Between diagonal rows, twist each pair three times.

1 *Half stitch through three pairs to the left and put up pin **1**.

2 Work through two pairs to the right in half stitch and put up pin **2**.**

3 Repeat from * to **.

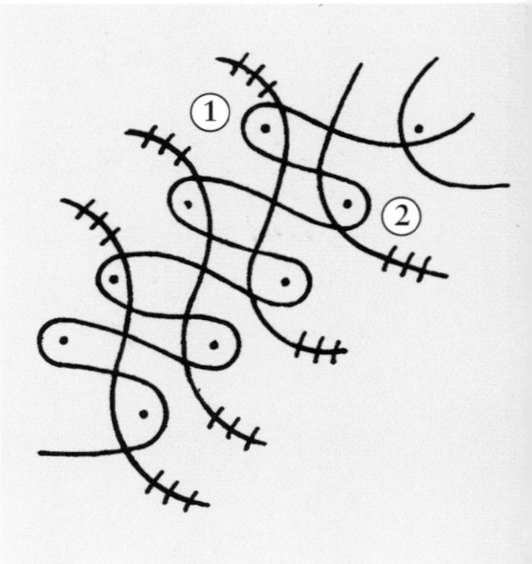

BIAS GROUND 2 (Fig 10.21)

Work in diagonal rows. Between diagonal rows, twist each pair three times.

Fig 10.20 Bias ground 1.

155

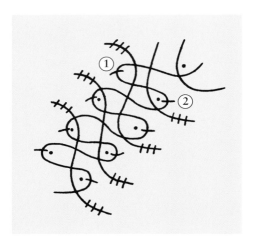

Fig 10.21
Bias ground 2.

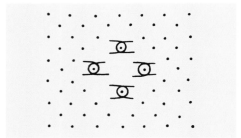

Fig 10.23 Compound spiders shown on the pricking.

1 *Cloth stitch through three pairs to the left, twist the workers and put up pin **1**.

2 Work through two pairs to the right in cloth stitch, twist the workers and put up pin **2**.**

3 Repeat from * to **.

COMPOUND SPIDERS
(Fig 10.22 and 10.23)

Work continuous spiders (see page 22) without ground stitches between them. There is no need for extra twists on the legs between the spiders.

Fig 10.22 BELOW
Compound spiders.

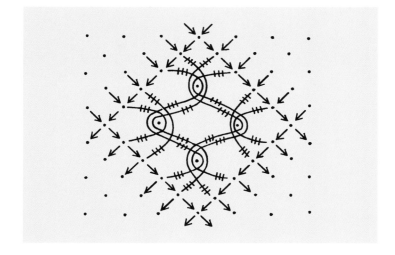

EYED SPIDER
(Figs 10.24 and 10.25)

This example of an eyed spider has four legs from left and right. Others may have more or fewer legs, but the principle of working is the same. The spider is worked with the eight pairs from pins **1** to **8**.

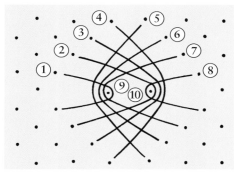

Fig 10.24 Eyed spider.

1 Twist all the pairs three times.

2 *Work the pair from pin **4** to the right through three pairs in cloth stitch.

3 Work the pair from pin **3** to the right through three pairs in cloth stitch.

4 Work the pair from pin **2** to the right through three pairs in cloth stitch.**

5 Work the pair from pin **1** to the right through three pairs in cloth stitch and put up pin **9**.

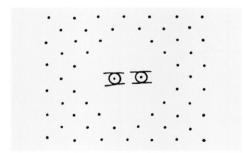

Fig 10.25 Eyed spider as shown on the pricking.

6 Work back to the left through three pairs in cloth stitch.

7 Work the pair from pin **8** to the left through three pairs in cloth stitch and put up pin **10**.

8 Work back to the right through three pairs in cloth stitch.

9 Repeat from * to ** and twist each pair three times.

ROUND SPIDER
(Figs 10.26 and 10.27)

In this example of a round spider there are four legs from each side.

1 Twist each pair twice.

2 Cloth stitch the top two pairs and pin up at **1**. Cover the pin with cloth stitch and twist.

3 Work the left pair at pin **1** to the left through three pairs in cloth stitch and twist.

4 Work the right pair at pin **1** to the right through three pairs in cloth stitch and twist.

5 Pin up under the workers on each side at pins **2** and **3**. Leave uncovered.

6 Twist the other six pairs once more and then work a spider's body in cloth

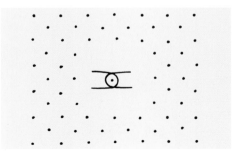

Fig 10.26 ABOVE Round spider.

Fig 10.27 LEFT Round spider as shown on the pricking.

stitch (three left pairs through three right pairs). Pin up at **4**, and complete the body (three left pairs through three right pairs). Twist each of these six pairs twice.

7 With the workers left at pins **2** and **3**, work in cloth stitch and twist through the three spider's legs on either side, and work together in cloth stitch.

8 Pin up between them at **5** and cover with a cloth stitch and twist.

9 Give all eight pairs one twist.

SMALL HOLE IN CLOTH STITCH (Figs 10.28 and 10.29)

1 Work the diamond in cloth stitch to pin **1**.

2 Take the workers back to the left through four pairs and put up pin **2**.

3 Cover the pin with cloth stitch. Both these pairs are now the workers for each side.

4 At pin **3**, the workers come together in cloth stitch. Put up the pin.

5 Cover the pin with cloth stitch. The right pair becomes a passive and the left pair are now the workers that complete the cloth shape. Work to the left to pin **4** first.

CLOTH STITCH DIAMOND WITH HOLE (Fig 10.30)

1 Work cloth stitch to pin **1**, bringing in one pair from each side.

2 Pin up at **1** and work to the left through four pairs, then put up pin **2**. Twist the next pair to the left and put up pin **3** under it. This pair is now the worker pair for the left side.

3 Work the left side to pin **4**, and leave uncovered.

4 Work the right side to pin **5** and leave uncovered.

5 Twist the pairs from pins **2** and **3** and work them together in cloth stitch and twist. Put up pin **6** and cover with cloth stitch and twist.

6 Work the worker pair at pin **5** to the left through four pairs and put up pin **7**. Leave it uncovered to become a passive pair.

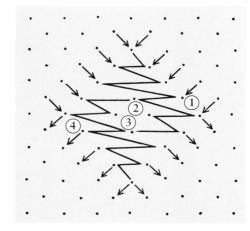

Fig 10.28 Small hole in cloth stictch.

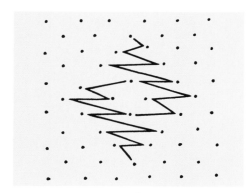

Fig 10.29 Small hole in cloth stitch as shown on the pricking.

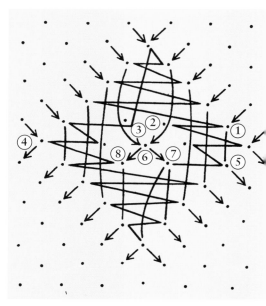

Fig 10.30 Cloth stitch diamond with hole.

7 Work the worker pair at pin **4** to the right through five pairs and put up pin **8**. This is now the worker pair that completes the cloth stitch diamond.

BRABANT STITCH (HONEYCOMB)
(Figs 10.31 and 10.32)

Work the pinholes in number order. All the pinholes are worked. Work the stitch as follows:

Half stitch, pin, half stitch and twist.

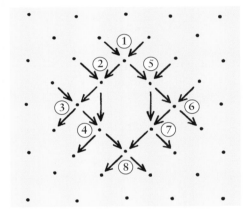

Fig 10.31 Brabant stitch (honeycomb).

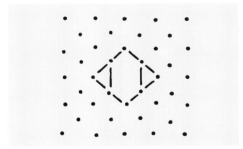

Fig 10.32 Brabant stitch as shown on the pricking.

TORCHON MAYFLOWER
(Fig 10.33)

This pattern consists of small cloth stitch diamonds surrounded by Brabant honeycomb stitch (see page 159).

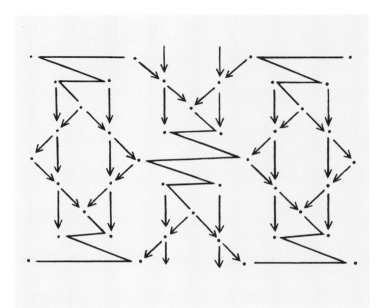

Fig 10.33 Torchon mayflower.

TWISTED HOLE GROUND
(Fig 10.34)

This ground stitch is worked in diagonal rows with pairs coming to each pinhole at an angle of 45°. Each pinhole is worked with two pairs. Work the stitch as follows:

Half stitch and twist, pin, half stitch and twist.

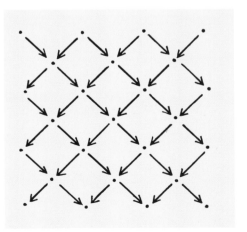

Fig 10.34 Twisted hole ground.

CANE GROUND
(Figs 10.35 and 10.36)
Work the stitch in number order, in cloth stitch and twist throughout.

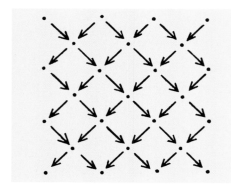

Fig 10.35 Cane ground.

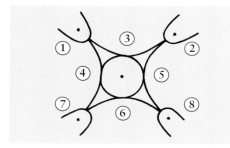

Fig 10.36 Working cane ground.

TRIANGULAR GROUND
(Figs 10.37 and 10.38)
Follow Fig 10.37 carefully.

1 Work the pairs from pins **1** and **2** in cloth stitch. Put up pin **3** between them. *Do not cover.*

2 Work the pair from **4** in cloth stitch through three pairs to the left and put up pin **5**.

3 Cover pin **5** with a cloth stitch, and twist the left pair once.

4 Work the right pair at pin **5** to the right through two pairs in cloth stitch, twist the workers once and leave.

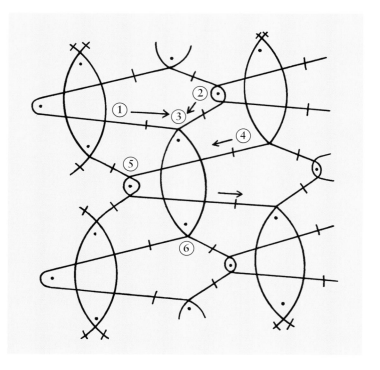

Fig 10.37
Triangular
ground.

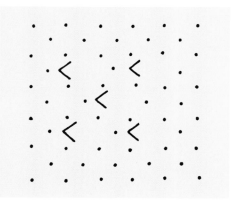

Fig 10.38
Triangular
ground as shown
on the pricking.

5 Pin up at **6** between the two pairs to the left of the workers, and cover pin **6** with a cloth stitch and twist.

WOVEN STITCH
(Figs 10.39 and 10.40)
Work this stitch within a surround of Torchon ground stitch.

1 Work the top left and right diagonal rows in Torchon ground.

160

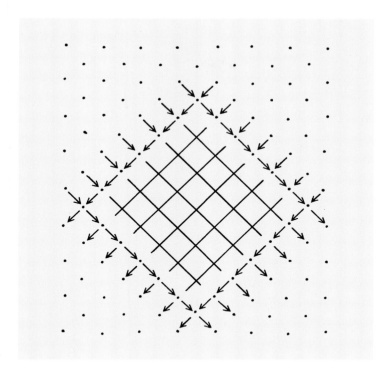

Fig 10.39 Woven stitch.

2 Work all the left pairs through all the right pairs in cloth stitch, starting at the top.

3 Complete the shape by working the bottom left and right diagonal rows in Torchon ground.

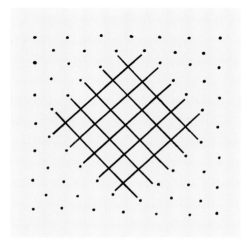

Fig 10.40 Woven stitch as shown on the pricking.

ADDITIONAL TECHNIQUES

MOVING LACE ON THE PILLOW

When work reaches the bottom of the pricking, you will need to move the lace to the top again in order to continue working. To do this, the bobbins are wrapped and pinned in the cover cloth, the tension is taken off the work, the pins are removed, and the work is pinned again to the top of the pricking.

In more detail, this is how it is done. Thread the bobbins onto knitting stitch-holders, unpin the cover cloth and wrap the bobbins in it. Pin the bobbins securely in the cloth. Move the parcel of bobbins up the pillow to remove the tension from the threads and pin it to the pillow. Very carefully remove all the pins from the pricking. Move the lace to the top of the pricking and replace at least a 2in (5cm) run of pins above the bobbins. Pay particular attention to the footside edges, as they can very easily be pulled up by mistake.

Moving lace is a laborious and time-consuming task. Nowadays, block pillows avoid the problem as the lace is worked over block sections of the pillow which can be moved up, or turned, as the work progresses. In this way, corners and long lengths of lace can be worked easily. A roller pillow is an alternative to the block pillow for long lengths.

EXTENDING A PATTERN

To extend a lace pattern, first photocopy it several times. Cut the patterns in such a way that they can be joined without missing pinholes, to make a continuous pattern. Make your pricking from this extended pattern.

REDUCING A PATTERN

Using a photocopy of the pattern, cut out repeats without missing pinholes and rejoin to make a continuous pattern. Make your pricking from this reduced pattern.

DESIGNING ON A SMALL SCALE (Fig 10.41)

When designing small patterns for the dolls' house, you will need to plot out the design onto graph paper. Use a metric grid marked out in 1mm, 5mm and 1cm divisions. Draw in blocks of pattern in pencil and then fill in the ground dots on the intersections of the lines. When you are happy with the design, mark it out with a fine marker pen. Place tracing paper over the graph paper and dot out the pattern again. This is your master copy. From this tracing paper, make your pricking. If you want to save the tracing paper copy, photocopy it and make the pricking from this (it will not be quite as accurate, because the photocopier stretches the design very slightly).

For mini patterns, plot the dots in the centre of each square as well as on the

intersection of the lines. This requires patience, a steady hand and good light. Reduction of standard patterns on a photocopier is another way of achieving small patterns but, as explained above, this can be inaccurate.

ATTACHING LACE TO FABRIC (Fig 10.42)

Choose fine, lightweight fabrics and iron before starting. Cut the fabric larger than the lace, then pin and tack the lace to it about three pinholes away from the footside edge.

Using a blunt-ended needle (no 24 tapestry) that will not split the threads, sew the lace to the material through the footside pinholes, using a three-sided stitch. Because each side of the stitch is worked twice, this is an extremely strong way of attaching lace to fabric. Following Fig 10.42, start with the needle on the wrong side.

- Bring the needle up at **A**, take it in at **B** and out again at **A**.
- Take the needle in at **B** and out at **C**, three times.
- Take the needle in at **A** and out at **C**.
- Take the needle in at **A** and out at **D**, three times.
- Take the needle in at **C** and out at **D**.
- Take the needle in at **C** and out at **E**, and so on.

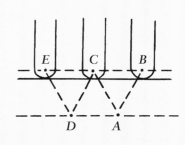

Fig 10.42 *Three-sided stitch.*

Pull each stitch to create a little hole in the fabric, but not so tight as to pucker the work. Hold the lace taut while working in order to prevent this. When you have finished, remove the tacking stitches, cut away the surplus fabric from the back (take care not to cut the lace), and overcast the edges on the wrong side.

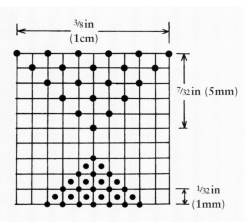

Fig 10.41 **Designing on a small scale.**

SUPPLIERS

MINIATURE HABERDASHERY

Dolls' House Draper
PO Box 128
Lightcliffe
Halifax
West Yorkshire
HX3 8RN

Tel: 01422 201275

HANDBAG FRAME AND FAN STICKS

Dear Dolly
Unit 12 Hodgson Court
Wickford
Essex
SS11 8XR

Tel: 01268 561267

GENERAL LACE AND EMBROIDERY SUPPLIES

Tim Parker
124 Corhampton Road
Bournemouth
Dorset
BH6 5NZ

Tel: 01202 429455

GENERAL LACE SUPPLIES

duchesse pins
of fine thread.

DJ Hornsby
25 Manwood Avenue
Canterbury
Kent
CT2 7AH

Tel: 01227 454605

LACE BOBBINS

C & D Springett
21 Hillmorton Road
Rugby
Warwickshire
CV22 5DF

Tel: 01788 544691

The Lace Guild
The Hollies
53 Audnam
Stourbridge
West Midlands
DY8 4AE

Tel: 01384 390739

ABOUT THE AUTHOR

Roz Snowden has lived most of her life in Kent.

For many years, she worked for the Greater London Council and her local district council as a cartographer.

Her artistic background, and interest in crafts, led Roz to bobbin lacemaking. She is a member of the Lace Guild, the Lace Society, and the Lacemakers' Circle, and she is an active member of her local lace group. She has exhibited and demonstrated lacemaking at many local events.

A Christmas present of a dolls' house led Roz to join several local miniaturist clubs and she soon realized she could adapt her lacemaking to 1/12th scale for her dolls' house. She now develops her own designs and patterns, and teaches miniature bobbin lace.

Roz sells her lace and patterns, and further details can be obtained from Roz at 4 Oldbury Close, Spring Lane, Ightham, Kent TN15 9DJ.

INDEX

TITLES AVAILABLE FROM
GMC Publications

BOOKS

WOODWORKING

40 More Woodworking Plans & Projects	*GMC Publications*	Making Chairs and Tables	*GMC Publications*
Bird Boxes and Feeders for the Garden	*Dave Mackenzie*	Making Fine Furniture	*Tom Darby*
Complete Woodfinishing	*Ian Hosker*	Making Little Boxes from Wood	*John Bennett*
Electric Woodwork	*Jeremy Broun*	Making Shaker Furniture	*Barry Jackson*
Furniture & Cabinetmaking Projects	*GMC Publications*	Pine Furniture Projects for the Home	*Dave Mackenzie*
Furniture Projects	*Rod Wales*	Sharpening Pocket Reference Book	*Jim Kingshott*
Furniture Restoration (Practical Crafts)	*Kevin Jan Bonner*	Sharpening: The Complete Guide	*Jim Kingshott*
Furniture Restoration and Repair for Beginners	*Kevin Jan Bonner*	Stickmaking: A Complete Course	*Andrew Jones & Clive George*
Green Woodwork	*Mike Abbott*	Woodfinishing Handbook (Practical Crafts)	*Ian Hosker*
The Incredible Router	*Jeremy Broun*	Woodworking Plans and Projects	*GMC Publications*
Making & Modifying Woodworking Tools	*Jim Kingshott*	The Workshop	*Jim Kingshott*

WOODTURNING

Adventures in Woodturning	*David Springett*	Practical Tips for Turners & Carvers	*GMC Publications*
Bert Marsh: Woodturner	*Bert Marsh*	Practical Tips for Woodturners	*GMC Publications*
Bill Jones' Notes from the Turning Shop	*Bill Jones*	Spindle Turning	*GMC Publications*
Bill Jones' Further Notes from the Turning Shop	*Bill Jones*	Turning Miniatures in Wood	*John Sainsbury*
Colouring Techniques for Woodturners	*Jan Sanders*	Turning Wooden Toys	*Terry Lawrence*
The Craftsman Woodturner	*Peter Child*	Understanding Woodturning	*Ann & Bob Phillips*
Decorative Techniques for Woodturners	*Hilary Bowen*	Useful Techniques for Woodturners	*GMC Publications*
Essential Tips for Woodturners	*GMC Publications*	Useful Woodturning Projects	*GMC Publications*
Faceplate Turning	*GMC Publications*	Woodturning: A Foundation Course	*Keith Rowley*
Fun at the Lathe	*R.C. Bell*	Woodturning: A Source Book of Shapes	*John Hunnex*
Illustrated Woodturning Techniques	*John Hunnex*	Woodturning Jewellery	*Hilary Bowen*
Intermediate Woodturning Projects	*GMC Publications*	Woodturning Masterclass	*Tony Boase*
Keith Rowley's Woodturning Projects	*Keith Rowley*	Woodturning Techniques	*GMC Publications*
Make Money from Woodturning	*Ann & Bob Phillips*	Woodturning Tools & Equipment Test Reports	*GMC Publications*
Multi-Centre Woodturning	*Ray Hopper*	Woodturning Wizardry	*David Springett*
Pleasure and Profit from Woodturning	*Reg Sherwin*		

WOODCARVING

The Art of the Woodcarver	*GMC Publications*	Understanding Woodcarving in the Round	*GMC Publications*
Carving Birds & Beasts	*GMC Publications*	Useful Techniques for Woodcarvers	*GMC Publications*
Carving on Turning	*Chris Pye*	Wildfowl Carving - Volume 1	*Jim Pearce*
Carving Realistic Birds	*David Tippey*	Wildfowl Carving - Volume 2	*Jim Pearce*
Decorative Woodcarving	*Jeremy Williams*	The Woodcarvers	*GMC Publications*
Essential Tips for Woodcarvers	*GMC Publications*	Woodcarving: A Complete Course	*Ron Butterfield*
Essential Woodcarving Techniques	*Dick Onians*	Woodcarving: A Foundation Course	*Zoë Gertner*
Lettercarving in Wood: A Practical Course	*Chris Pye*	Woodcarving for Beginners	*GMC Publications*
Practical Tips for Turners & Carvers	*GMC Publications*	Woodcarving Tools & Equipment Test Reports	*GMC Publications*
Understanding Woodcarving	*GMC Publications*	Woodcarving Tools, Materials & Equipment	*Chris Pye*

UPHOLSTERY

Seat Weaving (Practical Crafts)	*Ricky Holdstock*	Upholstery Restoration	*David James*
Upholsterer's Pocket Reference Book	*David James*	Upholstery Techniques & Projects	*David James*
Upholstery: A Complete Course	*David James*		

TOYMAKING

Designing & Making Wooden Toys	*Terry Kelly*	Making Wooden Toys & Games	*Jeff & Jennie Loader*
Fun to Make Wooden Toys & Games	*Jeff & Jennie Loader*	Restoring Rocking Horses	*Clive Green & Anthony Dew*
Making Board, Peg & Dice Games	*Jeff & Jennie Loader*	Wooden Toy Projects	*GMC Publications*

DOLLS' HOUSES AND MINIATURES

Architecture for Dolls' Houses *Joyce Percival*
Beginners' Guide to the Dolls' House Hobby *Jean Nisbett*
The Complete Dolls' House Book *Jean Nisbett*
Dolls' House Bathrooms: Lots of Little Loos *Patricia King*
Easy to Make Dolls' House Accessories *Andrea Barham*
Make Your Own Dolls' House Furniture *Maurice Harper*
Making Dolls' House Furniture *Patricia King*
Making Georgian Dolls' Houses *Derek Rowbottom*
Making Miniature Oriental Rugs & Carpets *Meik & Ian McNaughton*

Making Period Dolls' House Accessories *Andrea Barham*
Making Period Dolls' House Furniture *Derek & Sheila Rowbottom*
Making Tudor Dolls' Houses *Derek Rowbottom*
Making Unusual Miniatures *Graham Spalding*
Making Victorian Dolls' House Furniture *Patricia King*
Miniature Bobbin Lace *Roz Snowden*
Miniature Needlepoint Carpets *Janet Granger*
The Secrets of the Dolls' House Makers *Jean Nisbett*

CRAFTS

A Beginners' Guide to Rubber Stamping *Brenda Hunt*
Celtic Knotwork Designs *Sheila Sturrock*
Collage from Seeds, Leaves and Flowers *Joan Carver*
Complete Pyrography *Stephen Poole*
Creating Knitwear Designs *Pat Ashforth & Steve Plummer*
Creative Embroidery Techniques Using Colour Through Gold
Daphne J. Ashby & Jackie Woolsey
Cross Stitch Kitchen Projects *Janet Granger*
Cross Stitch on Colour *Sheena Rogers*
Embroidery Tips & Hints *Harold Hayes*

An Introduction to Crewel Embroidery *Mave Glenny*
Making Character Bears *Valerie Tyler*
Making Greetings Cards for Beginners *Pat Sutherland*
Making Knitwear Fit *Pat Ashforth & Steve Plummer*
Needlepoint: A Foundation Course *Sandra Hardy*
Pyrography Handbook (Practical Crafts) *Stephen Poole*
Tassel Making for Beginners *Enid Taylor*
Tatting Collage *Lindsay Rogers*
Temari: A Traditional Japanese Embroidery Technique
Margaret Ludlow

THE HOME

Home Ownership: Buying and Maintaining *Nicholas Snelling*

Security for the Householder:
Fitting Locks and Other Devices *E. Phillips*

VIDEOS

Drop-in and Pinstuffed Seats *David James*
Stuffover Upholstery *David James*
Elliptical Turning *David Springett*
Woodturning Wizardry *David Springett*
Turning Between Centres: The Basics *Dennis White*
Turning Bowls *Dennis White*
Boxes, Goblets and Screw Threads *Dennis White*
Novelties and Projects *Dennis White*
Classic Profiles *Dennis White*

Twists and Advanced Turning *Dennis White*
Sharpening the Professional Way *Jim Kingshott*
Sharpening Turning & Carving Tools *Jim Kingshott*
Bowl Turning *John Jordan*
Hollow Turning *John Jordan*
Woodturning: A Foundation Course *Keith Rowley*
Carving a Figure: The Female Form *Ray Gonzalez*
The Router: A Beginner's Guide *Alan Goodsell*
The Scroll Saw: A Beginner's Guide *John Burke*

MAGAZINES

WOODTURNING ◆ WOODCARVING ◆ FURNITURE & CABINETMAKING
THE ROUTER ◆ THE DOLLS' HOUSE MAGAZINE
CREATIVE CRAFTS FOR THE HOME ◆ BUSINESSMATTERS

◆

The above represents a full list of all titles currently published or scheduled to be published. All are available direct from the Publishers or through bookshops, newsagents and specialist retailers. To place an order, or to obtain a complete catalogue, contact:

GMC Publications,
166 High Street, Lewes, East Sussex BN7 1XU, United Kingdom
Tel: 01273 488005 Fax: 01273 478606

Orders by credit card are accepted